HOW TO TEACH
ASCENSION CLASSES

JOSHUA DAVID STONE, Ph.D.

HOW TO TEACH ASCENSION CLASSES

Joshua David Stone, Ph.D.

THE EASY-TO-READ ENCYCLOPEDIA of the SPIRITUAL PATH

✦ Volume XII ✦

Published by
Light Technology Publishing

© 1998 by Joshua David Stone, Ph.D.

Cover design by
Fay Richards

ISBN 1-891824-15-5

Published by
Light Technology Publishing
P.O. Box 1526
Sedona, AZ 86339
(800) 450-0985

Printed by
MI**SS**ION
PO**SS**IBLE
COMMERCIAL
PRINTING
P.O. Box 1495
Sedona, AZ 86339

Volumes in the series
The Easy-to-Read Encyclopedia of the Spiritual Path
by Joshua David Stone, Ph.D.
published by Light Technology

1. THE COMPLETE ASCENSION MANUAL
   How to Achieve Ascension in This Lifetime

2. SOUL PSYCHOLOGY
   Keys to Ascension

3. BEYOND ASCENSION
   How to Complete the Seven Levels of Initiation

4. HIDDEN MYSTERIES
   ETs, Ancient Mystery Schools and Ascension

5. THE ASCENDED MASTERS LIGHT THE WAY
   Beacons of Ascension

6. COSMIC ASCENSION
   Your Cosmic Map Home

7. A BEGINNER'S GUIDE TO THE PATH OF ASCENSION

8. GOLDEN KEYS TO ASCENSION AND HEALING
   Revelations of Sai Baba and the Ascended Masters

9. MANUAL FOR PLANETARY LEADERSHIP

10. YOUR ASCENSION MISSION
    Embracing Your Puzzle Piece

11. REVELATIONS OF A MELCHIZEDEK INITIATE

12. HOW TO TEACH ASCENSION CLASSES

13. ASCENSION AND ROMANTIC RELATIONSHIPS

Dedication

I dedicate this book to the beloved inner-plane ascended masters whom I'll lovingly call the Core 21. These masters, who have guided me in the writing of this book, are Melchizedek, Mahatma, Metatron, Divine Mother, Sai Baba, Helios and Vesta, Lord Buddha, Lord Maitreya, Quan Yin, Virgin Mary, Isis, Lakshmi, El Morya, Kuthumi, Serapis Bey, Paul the Venetian, Hilarion, Sananda, Saint Germain and Djwhal Khul. May their sacred and blessed energy flow through this book and into your lives.

Contents

A Request from the Spiritual and Cosmic Hierarchy

Beloved reader, you hold this book in your hand because you are one among many who have heard the call of the new millennium. This is a call to leadership and to uphold your rod of power, wear your mantle of self-mastery and share the path of God with your brothers and sisters on Earth. As one millennium passes to the next, we speak in unison the actions put forth by our beloved brother during his ministry as the Christ: "Oh thou that tellest good tidings to Zion, get ye up into the high mountain." The mountain, dear hearts, is the mountain of ascension and this dawn of the seventh golden age is calling forward all who would stand firm and strong upon that mountain and, with love, help guide their brothers and sisters up the path into the glory of their own ascension so that the kingdom of God be manifest on the Earth.

This is the hour of transformation and many are the ascended masters, angels, archangels and brethren from other worlds who wait for your simplest request to serve you in ever greater capacities. This is the hour to stand forth and know beyond a shadow of a doubt that you are not alone. In fact, the subtle presence of the higher realms has led you to pick up this book you now hold in your hands and calls you to action. This is not the hour for timidity or shyness to hold you back or for you to wait for total clarity. You have found this book and it has found you, because you are ready to help anchor heaven on Earth. You are clear enough, beloved pilgrim, to gather your fellow travelers around you so that you may help assist one another up the mountain of ascension into the rarefied air of full God realization.

Within these pages are practical tools and guidelines. The path has been forged for you, beloveds of God's heart. The road has been cleared and the way uncluttered. All you need do is follow the simple tools and guidance unfolded here, and you will be enabled to unfold all the love, wisdom and power that lies within you and your fellow travelers.

We of the celestial realms, we of the inner-plane hierarchy of planetary and cosmic ascended masters, we of the angelic and archangelic line, await your willingness to serve. Likewise do we call you forth. In unison we sound forth the call to let go of any imagined obstacles or self-imposed limitations or discomfort. If you feel the force of God moving within you and seek to share that divine energy, then you will follow the inner light that guided you to these pages, and in groups of two, three, four, twenty, fifty or hundreds you will join with us in helping to guide all to their greatest glory.

You have taken the first step toward the manifestation of this divine vision by picking up this book and reading thus far. You have heard the call and a road map is unfolded within the ensuing pages. Do not wait until the hour of perfection, for that hour shall never come—it will only be recognized. You are perfect now and ready now. All further journeys lead but to greater realization of this fact. Have the courage and the will to forge ahead, to answer our call and the call of your brothers and sisters who wait for you to pick up your mantle of leadership so that they may pick up their own.

We give you our solemn vow that we are ever by your side and there shall we remain to guide you, as you in turn help to gently guide others. Fear not, oh beloveds, and heed the call. Our prayer remains what it has been in the millennium past: "Oh, thou that tellest good tidings to Zion (yea, to humanity), get thee up into the high mountain." We await your arrival and accompany you in your journey.

Introduction

My beloved readers, it has been my great joy to put together this book to facilitate your process of teaching classes and workshops. I have put great thought into writing it and have spent many hours discussing this process with the masters.

One of my main reasons for writing this 18-volume series was to consolidate the best spiritual information from the past, present and future in Earth's history into one easy-to-read and practical set of books. This is why I have called it *The Easy-to Read Encyclopedia of the Spiritual Path.*

By the time I am complete with this project there may be as many as 50 volumes, which will cover everything a person needs to know to achieve self-realization and God realization on all levels. What is unique about these books is their comprehensiveness, practicality and easy-to-read style.

These books serve as an ideal foundation for teaching classes and doing workshops. The inner-plane ascended masters have guided me to put together this book, using the encyclopedia as its foundation. I want you, my beloved readers, to realize that it is not necessary to reinvent the wheel. I have purposely written these books to consolidate psychological and spiritual information on the cutting edge and integrate it with the best contributions from all spiritual paths and religions.

I have done the legwork and homework for you, which has been my joy. With the help of the masters I have outlined an entire one- to two-year program of classes you can teach. I have made this incredibly easy for you. When I suggest that you use this material to teach classes, it could be for two, five, ten or even a hundred people. The number doesn't matter. I even recommend doing this program with a friend in a type of ascension "buddy system" if you like.

I encourage you to consider setting up a class in your home. You could lead it, or it could be a leaderless class where group members take turns. If you are reading this book it means you are ready. Part of the responsibility of moving into higher levels of initiation is that the higher you go, the more leadership and responsibility is placed on you by God and the masters.

Teaching or setting up a class in your home to facilitate ascension realization is one of the most important services you could offer your friends, students and even family. With this book I have made it easy. I show in detail how to start and how to end every class. I have laid out the structure of each class for almost two years. I have shared with you here how to celebrate the major holy days that the inner-plane ascended masters would like us to celebrate on Earth.

Using my teaching experience, I have also outlined all the logistical and third-dimensional considerations that will come up. I have put deep thought into this book, with the help of the masters, so that you can teach a class for an entire year with little extra homework. The only tools you would need would be a certain number of my books and my ten meditation tapes.

You have my total permission to use and photocopy for both yourself and class members all the material in my published books and manuscripts as long as you give due credit. I have structured every aspect of these classes with the latest spiritual and psychological tools, meditations, prayers and ascension activations this world has ever known. All you have to do is gather the people and begin. I guarantee you that these classes will be some of the most profound classes taught on Earth.

I am paid nothing for this except the knowledge that lightworkers in every country in the world are being accelerated in the process of achieving their ascension and liberation from the wheel of rebirth. I am enriched when people move from suffering to a joy and inner peace that passeth understanding. The masters and I, as they stated so eloquently in the opening section, are now calling to lightworkers around the globe in every country and city on the planet to claim the rod of power and step forward in leadership to teach or offer your home for this program of ascension classes and/or discussion groups. You do not have to be the teacher; you could set it up as a discussion group with friends. How you do it is not important. Do whatever you intuitively feel is right. What is important is to take a risk. The number of people who come doesn't matter, for if only one person is helped, it is worth it.

The inner-plane ascended masters of the Planetary and Cosmic Hierarchy are now putting forth this request to lightworkers. Do not wait until you feel comfortable, for the law of the psyche is that if you wait until then, it will never happen. At some point you need to just do it. It is a little like "fake it till you make it."

The structure of the class guarantees success. If teaching or hosting a class does not feel right to you after reading through this book, you can try doing it with a friend. I guarantee it will be one of the most profound years of spiritual growth you have ever experienced. Maybe doing it with a friend will show you how easy it would be for you to set up a class in your area.

On that note let us move to the structural organization of the class to show you how easy it is.

1

Opening and Closing Your Classes

Opening a Class Session

After meditating and consulting with the masters, this is what we have come up with for the opening of a class session:

1. Clearing Negative Energies: The Burning Pot
2. Unifying the Group Energy: Holding Hands
3. Establishing the Ascension Column and Pillar of Light
4. Clearing with the Platinum Net
5. Axiatonal Alignment
6. The Ascension Flame
7. Invoking the Planetary and Cosmic Hierarchy
8. The Soul and Monad Mantras
9. Michael's Golden Dome of Protection
10. The Great Invocation
11. Three *Oms*
12. Optional Prayers (differing each week, such as the Lord's Prayer, Rosary, Saint Francis Prayer, Affirmation of the Disciple)

This is only the first ten minutes of your class, so I think you can already sense how powerful the class will be. This sequence of prayers, invocations and mantras will be the same for every class opening.

Let me now briefly go through each one of these to explain what you will be doing. Since this book is for teachers of all levels, the masters told me to be sure to explain the process for beginning to advanced teachers.

1 Clearing Negative Energies: The Burning Pot

I would recommend setting up the burning pot about five minutes before you officially begin the class. Everyone will be seated, and on the floor in the center of the room is a hot plate, on which is a little metal pot. You have already poured about a quarter inch of Epsom salts into the pot. As you are about to begin, pour no more than half an inch of rubbing alcohol over the Epsom salts. When everyone is quiet, throw a match into the rubbing alcohol. For about five minutes it will burn up all the etheric, astral and mental negative energy in the room. I call this the New Age campfire. Everyone in your group will love it. Explain its effects. I would also recommend that you light some sage or incense at this time.

2 Unifying the Group Energy: Holding Hands

When the pot burns out, the spiritual atmosphere of the entire room will be clear. Then guide the group to hold hands for one minute and connect with each other's heart chakras. This will unify the group consciousness.

3 Establishing the Ascension Column and Pillar of Light

The next step is to call the Planetary and Cosmic Spiritual Hierarchy to establish and activate a gigantic ascension column in the room. Ask that it be connected to a gigantic pillar of light and to your group's planetary and cosmic antakarana, the tube of light that connects you with your monad and God.

4 Clearing with the Platinum Net (see page 57)

Call forth to Melchizedek, the Mahatma and Metatron to bring down the platinum net through the entire group and your home. Platinum is the highest-frequency color available to Earth. The only higher frequency is the clear light of God, which has no color. The platinum net will clear the group and your home of all negative and imbalanced energies on *all* levels.

5 Axiatonal Alignment (see page 56)

The next step is to call again to the Planetary and Cosmic Hierarchy for a planetary and cosmic axiatonal alignment. This will balance all meridians of each individual and instantly align the group energy with God and the consciousness of the Spiritual Hierarchy on all levels.

6 The Ascension Flame

The next step in the class is to call to the Spiritual Hierarchy and inner-plane ascended masters to anchor and activate the golden white ascension flame. You will instantly feel and even see this energy coming in.

7 Invoking the Spiritual and Cosmic Hierarchy

The next step in the class is to call to the entire Spiritual and Cosmic Hierarchy to join your class. Ask that the appropriate master step forward to overlight this class. If there are particular masters you are connected with, this is the time to call them forward. If you like, you can also suggest that the group call forth the masters they would like to assist.

8 The Soul and Monad Mantras

The soul mantra was given by ascended master Djwhal Khul to the Earth through the channelings of Alice Bailey. In my opinion it is one of the most profound mantras on the planet and should be recited every time any spiritual work is about to be ignited. The original soul mantra goes as follows:

I am the Soul,
I am the Light Divine,
I am Love,
I am Will,
I am Fixed Design.

Since most of you, my beloved readers, have already passed your fourth initiation, it is appropriate to change the soul mantra to the monad mantra, the updated version. The word "monad" is simply substituted for "soul."

I am the Monad,
I am the Light Divine,
I am Love,
I am Will,
I am Fixed Design.

Actually, I recommend that you say both mantras in the order given. Saying them will ignite your higher self and mighty I Am Presence (monad) into action. (Try it, you'll like it!)

9 Michael's Golden Dome of Protection

The next step is to call for Archangel Michael and his legion of angels to create a golden dome of protection for the group. Archangel Michael serves on the first ray, and his specific function is to provide protection. You might also request protection for each member of the group in their spiritual paths and service work.

10 The Great Invocation

The next step is to recite the Great Invocation. (Have it printed out before your first class so that each member will have a copy.) This is a prayer given by Lord Maitreya, the planetary Christ, sometime between 1945 and 1950. It is one of the most powerful prayers ever given to lightworkers and the new group of World Servers. I will first give you the short version, then the longer version. I recommend doing the short version for most classes, but on special holy days the longer version. This mantra was obtained from the Alice Bailey book, *The Externalization of the Hierarchy*.

Short Version

From the point of Light within the Mind of God
Let Light stream forth into the minds of men.
Let Light descend on Earth.

From the point of Love within the Heart of God
Let Love stream forth into the hearts of men.
May Christ return to Earth.

From the center where the Will of God is known
Let purpose guide the little wills of men—
The purpose which the masters know and serve.

From the center which we call the race of men
Let the Plan of Love and Light work out
And may it seal the door where evil dwells.

Let Light and Love and Power restore the Plan on Earth.

Photocopy or type the following to put with the soul and monad mantras and possibly other prayers I will suggest.

Long Version*

Let the Forces of Light bring illumination to mankind,
Let the Spirit of Peace be spread abroad,
May men of goodwill everywhere meet in a spirit of cooperation,
May forgiveness on the part of all men
be the keynote at this time,
Let power attend the efforts of the Great Ones.
So let it be, and help us to do our part.

Let the Lords of Liberation issue forth,
Let them bring succor to the sons of men,
Let the Rider from the Secret Place come forth,
And coming, save.
Come forth, O Mighty One,

Let the souls of men awaken to the Light,
And may they stand with massed intent,
Let the fiat of the Lord go forth,
The end of woe has come!
Come forth, O Mighty One,
The hour of service of the Saving Force has now arrived.
Let it be spread abroad, O Mighty One.

Let Light and Love and Power and Death
Fulfill the purpose of the Coming One.
The will to save is here,
The love to carry forth the work is widely spread abroad,
The active aid of all who know the truth is also here.
Come forth, O Mighty One, and blend these three.

Construct a great defending wall,
The rule of evil now must end.

---

* This prayer is from Alice Bailey's *The Externalization of the Hierarchy*.

From the point of Light within the Mind of God
Let Light stream forth into the minds of men.
Let Light descend on Earth.

From the point of Love within the Heart of God
Let Love stream forth into the hearts of men.
May Christ return to Earth.

From the center where the Will of God is known
Let purpose guide the little wills of men—
The purpose which the masters know and serve.

From the center which we call the race of men
Let the Plan of Love and Light work out,
And may it seal the door where evil dwells.

Let Light and Love and Power restore the Plan on Earth.

11 Three Oms

Sounding the *Om* is always a wonderful way to attune with and activate the God force. It is also helpful in raising the vibrational frequencies before your prayers and the rest of the class.

12 Optional Prayers

The next step would be to choose a new prayer each week to end the opening 10 minutes. The masters again recommended the Lord's Prayer, the Rosary, the Prayer of Saint Francis and/or the Affirmation of the Disciple, which is a prayer channeled by Djwhal Khul through Alice Bailey. Djwhal's prayer is a classic, one I think your group will enjoy on occasion. Feel free to add prayers of any religions or spiritual paths. If group members would like to share a favorite, that is another option. For your convenience I am including here the prayers I have mentioned, which you can photocopy as needed.

The Lord's Prayer

Our Father, who art in heaven, hallowed be thy name.
Thy kingdom come, thy will be done on Earth as it is in heaven.
Give us this day our daily bread,
and forgive us our debts as we forgive our debtors.
And lead us not into temptation, but deliver us from evil.
For thine is the kingdom and the power and the glory forever.
Amen.

Prayer of Saint Francis

Lord, make me an instrument of Your peace.
Where there is hatred, let me sow love.
Where there is injury, pardon;

where there is doubt, faith;
where there is despair, hope;
where there is darkness, light;
and where there is sadness, joy.

Divine master, grant that I may not so much seek to be
consoled as to console;
to be understood as to understand;
to be loved as to love; for it is in giving that we receive;
it is in pardoning that we are pardoned;
and it is in dying that we are born to eternal life.

Traditional Rosary

In the name of the Father and the Son and of the Holy Spirit.
Amen.

I believe in God, the Father Almighty,
Creator of Heaven and Earth;
and in Jesus Christ, His only Son, our Lord,
who was conceived by the Holy Spirit, born of the Virgin Mary,
suffered under Pontius Pilate,
was crucified, died and was buried.
He descended into hell;
the third day he arose again from the dead;
He ascended into heaven to sitteth at the right hand of God,
the Father Almighty; from thence he shall come to judge
the living and the dead.
I believe in the Holy Spirit, the Holy Catholic Church,
the communion of saints, the forgiveness of sins,
the resurrection of the body and life everlasting. Amen.

Our Father, who art in heaven, hallowed be thy name.
Thy kingdom come, Thy will be done on Earth as it is in heaven.
Give us this day our daily bread and forgive us our trespasses
as we forgive those who trespass against us.
And lead us not into temptation, but deliver us from evil. Amen.

Hail Mary, full of grace; the Lord is with thee.
Blessed art thou among women,
and blessed is the fruit of thy womb, Jesus.
Holy Mary, Mother of God, pray for us sinners
now and at the hour of our death. Amen.

Glory be to the Father and to the Son and to the Holy Spirit
as it was in the beginning, is now, and ever shall be,
world without end. Amen.

Hail, holy Queen, Mother of Mercy,
Our life, our sweetness, and our hope.
To thee do we cry, poor banished children of Eve;
to thee do we send up our signs,
mourning and weeping in this valley of tears.
Turn, then, most gracious advocate,
thine eyes of mercy toward us;
and after this, our exile, show unto us
the blessed fruit of thy womb, Jesus;
O clement, O loving, O sweet Virgin Mary.

Pray for us, O holy Mother of God,
That we may be made worthy of the promises of Christ.
O God, whose only begotten Son, by his life,
death and resurrection
has purchased for us the rewards of eternal life.
Grant, we beseech thee, that meditating upon these mysteries
in the most Holy Rosary of the Blessed Virgin Mary,
we may imitate what they contain,
and obtain what they promise,
through the same Christ our Lord. Amen.

A New Age Rosary*

First make the sign of the cross five times, honoring our Lord's five wounds.

Sorrowful and Immaculate Heart of Mary,
pray for us who seek refuge in thee.
Holy Mother, save us through your
Immaculate Heart's flame of love.

At the end, hold the cross and say three times:

Glory be to the Father, etc.

Close the rosary by saying:

Mother of God, send down your grace
through your Immaculate Heart's flame of love
to the whole human race, now and at the hour of our death.

Eternal Father-Mother God, I offer you the Body and Blood,
the Soul and Divinity of your dearly beloved Son,
Our Lord Jesus Christ, in atonement for our sins
and the sins of the whole world.

---

* From Earlyne Chaney's *A Book of Prophecy.*

For the sake of his most sorrowful Passion,
have mercy on us and the whole world.
Holy God, Holy Omnipotent One, Holy Immortal One,
have mercy on us and on the whole world.

The Affirmation of the Disciple*

I am a point of light within a greater light,
I am a strand of loving energy within the stream of love divine.
I am a point of sacrificial fire,
focused within the fiery will of God and thus I stand.
I am a way by which men may achieve,
I am a source of strength enabling them to stand.
I am a beam of light shining upon their way, and thus I stand.
And standing thus, revolve and tread this way, the ways of men,
And know the ways of God. And thus I stand.

I strive toward understanding.
Let wisdom take the place of knowledge in my life.
I strive toward cooperation.
Let the master of my life, the soul,
and likewise the one I seek to serve,
throw light through me on others.

In the center of the Will of God I stand.
Naught shall deflect my will from His.
I implement that will by love.
I turn toward the field of service.
I, the triangle divine, work out that will within the square
and serve my fellow men.

I am a messenger of Light.
I am a pilgrim on the way of Love.
I do not walk alone, but know myself as one with all great souls,
and one with them in service.
Their strength is mine. This strength I claim.
My strength is theirs and this I freely give.
A soul, I walk on Earth, I represent the One.

I am one with my group of brothers, and all that I have is theirs.
May the love which is in my soul pour forth to them.
May the strength which is in me lift and aid them.
May the thoughts which my soul creates
reach and encourage them.

---

* This affirmation is from Alice Bailey's *Ponder on This.*

I know the law, and toward the goal I strive.
Naught shall arrest my progress on the way.
Each tiny life within my form responds.
My soul has sounded forth that call,
and clearer day by day it sounds.

The glamour holds me not.
The path of light streams clear ahead.
My plea goes forth to reach the hearts of men.
I seek, I try to serve your need.
Give me your hand and tread the path with me.

The sons of men are one and I am one with them.
I seek to love, not hate.
I seek to serve and not exact due service.
I seek to heal, not hurt.

Let pain bring due reward of light and love.
Let the soul control the outer form and life and all events,
and bring to light the love
which underlies the happenings of the time.
Let vision come and insight.
Let the future stand revealed.
Let inner union demonstrate and outer cleavages be gone.
Let love prevail.
Let all men love.

We know, oh Lord, of life and love, about the need.
Touch our hearts anew with love, that we too may love and give.

These last four prayers are only options; please do not feel obligated to use them. You may have other prayers or ideas that are even better, or you may prefer to end the opening of the class after the three *Oms*.

I think you will see from the opening segment how powerful this class will be. So far this has taken 10 minutes.

Closing a Class Session

After consulting with the masters, we came up with the following closing. This is just a tentative format and will take 10 to 15 minutes. Trust your own intuition and creativity if you get new ideas or want to change things around. My role is to give you a basic structure to work with, but it is not written in stone (excuse the pun).

The masters and I recommend the following:

1. Clearing with the Platinum Net
2. Axiatonal Alignment
3. Removing the Core-Fear Matrix
4. Infusing Core Love and the Christ/Buddha Qualities
5. The Soul and Monad Mantras
6. Visiting the Golden Chamber of Melchizedek (see page 34)
   Group Prayer for Self and Others
   Prayers of Protection
   Prayer to Hold and Retain Energies
   Prayer for Ascension Acceleration
   Return and Grounding
7. Invoking a Golden Cylinder
8. Invoking Galactic Healers and Healing Angels
9. The Great Invocation
10. Three Oms
11. Prayer of Thanksgiving

1 Clearing with the Platinum Net (see page 57)

This was part of the opening and requesting it again will again clear away any negative or imbalanced energies released and cleansed during class.

2 Axiatonal Alignment (see page 56)

This ascension activation was also done at the opening; this time it will solidify the attunement and ensure that each group member leaves fully aligned.

3 Removing the Core-Fear Matrix* (see page 64)

This clearing program and dispensation from the Spiritual Hierarchy is extremely important for each closing. Removing the core-fear matrix is accomplished by a latticework of light that the inner-plane ascended masters anchor over each individual and which will highlight any imbalanced programming in your four-body system. The ascended masters have the ability to pull all fear-based programming, all negative-ego programming, all separative programming, right out of your field, like a gardener pulling weeds. Fear-based programming shows up under the latticework of a light-matrix removal as gray and black weeds intertwined throughout your subtle bodies. In each class session take at least 5 minutes for this. Ask the inner-plane masters to remove all the core fears and the programming of negative ego, self-centeredness and separation. If there are specific negative-ego qualities that you wish removed, this is a good time to request it. Then wait another 4 or 5 minutes and feel it being done.

---

* For more information on core-fear removal, read *Beyond Ascension*.

The group members will be able to feel these dark weeds being pulled out through the crown chakra. Doing this on an ongoing basis over many months will eventually clear these psychic weeds from your system, though you still have to do your consciousness work so they won't return. This is a new dispensation of the Spiritual Hierarchy; its value is beyond words. Also request that this work continue during the night.

4 Infusing Core Love and the Christ/Buddha Qualities

After 5 minutes of core-fear removal, the next step is to invoke an infusion of core love and the Christ/Buddha qualities. Ask the inner-plane ascended masters to bring forth a downpouring of core love infused with the Christ/Buddha qualities. Since the core fear or negative-ego programming has been largely removed, there is room for its replacement by the Christ/Buddha qualities. This is another gift of the masters to help infuse your subconscious mind and four-body system with these qualities. Then remain silent for four or five minutes to receive this blessing. Everyone will be able to feel it.

5 The Soul and Monad Mantras (see page 2)

The next step is to repeat the soul and monad mantras as from the opening. This will expand the aura and bring more light into it.

6 Visiting the Golden Chamber of Melchizedek (see page 34)

The next step is to ask the inner-plane ascended masters to bring forth a group merkabah, which is like a spiritual boat that will take the group to the Golden Chamber of Melchizedek and his ascension seat. Sit in the silence of this energy for a minute, and then ask the group to share any personal prayers they have for self or others at any level (physical healing, relationships, health, money problems, spiritual help and so on). Encourage them to not be shy, and be the first to share some of your personal prayer requests.

The Golden Chamber is one of the holiest places in the universe to visit. It is like the ultimate church. Encourage the class to share their prayers from the deepest part of heart and soul. Praying for others is also fine, and if you are inspired to pray for world conditions and events, that would also be appropriate.

The leader or chairperson for that week might also have a regular prayer for protection and for everyone's energy to be sealed in order to retain the attunement achieved in class. I recommend that you request an acceleration toward ascension and that the masters keep working with the group at night while you sleep.

The final prayer request in the Golden Chamber would be that the class be returned back to Earth in the group merkabah and into their physical bodies. Then request everyone to place their grounding cords back into the Earth.

7 Invoking a Golden Cylinder (see page 66)

The next step is to request the Spiritual Hierarchy to anchor a golden cylinder. This is a golden tube of light that is anchored around each individual, drawing out all negative or imbalanced energy like a magnet, so that each person will go home crystal clear in their subtle bodies. Take about one minute to do this.

8 Invoking Galactic Healers and Healing Angels

This invocation is a request to balance the chakras and body energy fields. This will ensure that all class members go home totally balanced. It is also a good idea to request each class member to inwardly ask the galactic healers and healing angels to work on any specific health lessons and continue this healing at night during sleep, assuming the member wishes it. (See also page 69.)

9 The Great Invocation

Recite together the Great Invocation (see p. 3-5).

10 Three *Oms*

Then chant three *Oms*.

11 Prayer of Thanksgiving

Beloved Father/Mother God, we thank you for this time together. We thank you for allowing our group to celebrate the divinity of all life, to share in the love of the heart of God and the light/wisdom within the mind of God. We thank you for assisting us in our ascension process and granting us the love, wisdom and power to live a life of service. In gratitude to you, Father/Mother God, both within and without, we ask to merge our wills with thine own, and thank you again for providing this precious time of communion, acceleration and sharing. Amen.

This will close the session.

Social and Networking Time

It is very important to allow some socializing and networking time after the session, even if just a half hour. This helps ground the energy and gives an opportunity for expressing love and sharing. Some spiritual groups focus on the vertical planes of life, ignoring the horizontal, but in my opinion this is not good. Integration and synthesis is always the key.

You can see the power in this closing structure. So far we have given the first ten minutes and the last fifteen minutes of the class. Are you getting a sense, my friends, of how successful this class will be if you claim your power and do it? Wait until you experience the real classes!

2

Logistical Considerations

I have brainstormed the following list of third-dimensional, logistical considerations with the masters, adding my own personal experiences in giving classes and lectures for the past twenty years. This comprehensive list should prove valuable to first-timers as well as experienced teachers. Sometimes these third-dimensional, logistical subtleties make all the difference for a successful class. My beloved readers, my brainstorming makes your job quite easy.

It is always a nice effect to light incense in the main room or the bathroom. Make sure there are matches there. Tell the group where the bathrooms are (it goes without saying that the bathrooms should be clean, as should the rest of the house). As Edgar Cayce's channelings of the Universal Mind said, "Make your earthly home a place where angels would choose to tread." Be sure there is enough toilet paper and an extra roll set out.

Be sure that when the class starts, all the phones are shut off. If there is a security door in your home that is connected to your phone, give one of the class members the responsibility for beeping classmates in upon arrival.

Set up a table in the back of the main room with a mailing list and a place for phone numbers. This list should be photocopied and given to the class members so that they can contact each other outside of class—if this is acceptable to class members. On this back table can be placed your flyers and/or business cards and those of your classmates.

It is also important to have available herb teas, instant coffee, honey, brown sugar, paper cups, a few healthy snacks and napkins.

Before starting your first class, make sure you have comfortable chairs and/or cushions to sit on. Have classmates bring their own cushions or pillows if they like. Make a decision about the cost of the class or discussion group before you begin. It can be free, or you might charge a small donation or a set class fee. I would recommend setting a basket on your back table or in the center of your circle with a cardboard sign saying "Donation," listing the cost. Some people take the approach of writing "Love Donation" and let people decide for themselves. There is no right or wrong way; it depends on how the class is structured.

Be sure to have in advance photocopies of the Great Invocation, the soul and monad mantras and the other prayers you will be using regularly. Class members can be instructed to leave the copy on their seats at the end of each session to keep copying costs down.

It is recommended that the classes falling on Wesak, the Festival of the Christ or the Festival of Humanity be free. On special holy days it might be nice to have a potluck before or after class. In the next chapter I will discuss the holy days that the inner-plane ascended masters recommend we celebrate each year, and how to celebrate them properly.

Another logistical consideration is the size of the class. Some of you may do this with a friend, some in a trinity, some with twelve people, some with twenty-five or more. This will depend on the space you have, the number of chairs and your personal preference. It must also be decided if this is to be an open or closed group. By this I mean, will new people be allowed to join on an ongoing basis, or do you have a set group of committed people you want to work with?

Another issue is what I call the *commitment factor*. Is this class or group going to be held on a drop-in basis, or do you want to set it up with each group member making a commitment to attend for a certain period of time? This commitment could be for four weeks, six weeks, three months or a year. My personal opinion is that the class will function better if the core group attendees have some kind of commitment to the process, especially in the beginning.

The next decision to be made is whether there will be one leader, no leader, or a rotating chairperson. If this is a class among friends, having one leader might not be appropriate. In my experience, because the class has been structured by the ascended masters, it is important that one person take charge to facilitate the process. It is essential that one person get the class started. Once it is ongoing, it is possible to share the leadership. However, it is not necessary or required. If your class is for the general public, a leader or facilitator is essential.

The next step is to decide how to gather together a class. It can be done through a group effort by a number of your friends, family or students. It might be helpful to put together a flyer with the titles of classes for a three-month period, which you can easily put together after reading this book. The flyer can be input on a computer by you or one of your friends. The other possibility is to place a small ad in one of the New Age/holistic newspapers in your area. Another easy way to advertise your class is to mention it on your phone machine or service, if this is comfortable and you are marketing it to the general public. If this class is going to be among friends or a small core group, this might not be appropriate. If the class gets too large for your home, you might consider renting a space once a week in a hotel, school or church. It is not very expensive and they would supply all the chairs you will need.

Put together a book list of those you will be using for the period your class will last. Some of the classes will involve reading certain sections of my books. If class members know the class schedule, they can bring their books with them. Otherwise, a single book will be passed around for members to read aloud, if they feel comfortable doing that. If the class expects to continue for a longer period, create a certificate of completion or have a friend skilled in computer work create one for you—for example, a nine-month training course on ascension. After a second course is completed, a higher-level ascension teacher-training certificate can be provided.

Always be sure to take a 10-minute break about halfway through for everyone to stretch, use the bathroom and get tea or a little snack. Tell the class members at the first meeting that people are welcome to use the bathroom during class.

Another skill that all teachers must develop is how to deal with disruptive people who occasionally attend. Forgiveness and patience is always the best course. However, if one member talks too much and monopolizes the group time, it is your job as the leader to politely, but in a firm and loving manner, thank the person for sharing and guide the conversation and sharing to other class members. If the disruption continues over time and affects the group, it may be your job to ask that member not to attend class. This would be done only in extreme cases. It is probably a good idea to consult privately a number of the core members in the group to get their feelings and thoughts about what is an appropriate action to take.

Always start the class on time, or no more than 5 minutes late. Class members should be told in advance of the class, and at the opening of the first meeting, that everyone is expected to arrive at least 15 minutes early. This is especially important at a class such as this because the beginning entails prayers and meditations. People who come in late interrupt the attunement and cohesiveness you are trying to establish before the session.

It is also important to end the class on time. A little flexibility is always important, but these classes usually occur in the evening. People have jobs in the morning and possibly have babysitters; they might be tired after a long day at work and so on. More is not always better. I have seen many people give good classes or workshops, but damage their effectiveness by not ending on time. It is like eating a meal. It is better to stop eating at the moment when there is the first sign of fullness. If you eat more than this, the energy dissipates and you often get sleepy. The same thing is true with spiritual digestion. Keep them coming back for more.

The leader of the group hosting the class also has what I call hosting responsibilities. There is a spiritual responsibility to help make everyone feel comfortable and at home when they arrive. It may be your job to introduce new people to the core members. It might be your job to speak to them during the break or when the class is over just to make them feel comfortable. I think you get the idea. It is also important at the first class to let the members know where they can get the books. You might know certain bookstores that carry them. They can order my books from me if their local metaphysical bookstore doesn't have them.

The supplies you need for this course are inexpensive. All you need are my ten meditation tapes and a set of my books, which I'm sure many of you readers already have. (New tapes are added after Wesak each year.) This book provides classes for almost two years. You can choose which classes you are most drawn to, and these will determine which books you need. All the meditations can be found in this book, but the reading part of the class sessions will necessitate using material from my books. (The total cost of the eight tapes is $110, and the books, sold locally, are $15 each. Manuscripts are $25 each plus $5 for postage and handling.) Class members do not need the tapes or even the books, only you, because I recommend no homework. Everyone should participate in the reading part of the class, passing around *your* book. The information supplied in my series is the equivalent of hundreds of books and tapes, which are at the cutting edge in the field of spirituality, psychology and physical healing.

Something that could bring greater closeness among class members is a field trip to the annual Wesak celebration in Mount Shasta, California, where 1400 to 3000 disciples, initiates and ascended beings gather. You might consider it. Your group could then connect with other groups doing similar work around the globe.

Once you have decided to set up a class or discussion group, go through these two chapters again and make an outline of the things you need to do. If you follow my simple instructions, in four hours you can set up a three-month course and have everything organized in your mind. You will need one list for things to do in advance of the class and a second list of things to say and do during the class. Many things on the second list have to be done only for the first class. Once you have an outline for that initial class, you can relax because it will all be on paper.

Another responsibility of the leader is to keep an eye on the time to make sure the reading, sharing, prayers and meditations aren't too long. Sometimes, because of interest and your immersion in the spiritual energies, it is easy to forget the time. Someone in the group needs to take responsibility to keep things moving and make sure the class doesn't go on too long—or too short, for that matter.

The leader of the group, especially in the beginning, should encourage people to call one another socially or professionally for spiritual support or as ascension buddies, possibly to meditate together on the phone and do ascension activations.

For close-knit groups there is also the possibility of doing service projects or volunteer work together once a month or more. Some ideas you might consider: feeding the homeless, hospice work, helping the mentally challenged or physically handicapped, big brother/big sister, teaching people to read and singing in nursing homes or hospitals. The potential ways to serve are endless.

3

Mantras and Power Names of God

Here is a list of mantras and power names of God. You can use this material in your classes if you like. Chanting or repeating the names of God is a powerful tool of spiritual growth and attunement. The names of God, mantras and words of power from all religions can be used at your discretion.

Mantras from the Mystical Jewish Tradition

1. **Elohim** (the divine Mother aspect of God, All that God Is; in my opinion, this is one of the most powerful mantras there is)
2. **Yod Hay Vod Hay** or **Yod Hay Wah Hay** (the divine Father aspect of God; it could also be chanted using Christian terminology, *Jehovah*)
3. **Adonai** (the Earth aspect of God; in the Kabbalah it means Lord)
4. **Eh Hay Eh** (the I Am; another version perhaps even more powerful is **Ehyeh Asher Ehyeh**, I Am That I Am, the name given to Moses by God when he spoke to the burning bush)
5. **YHWH** (the living, revealed name of God behind all the creator gods)
6. **El Shaddai** (God Almighty)
7. **Ha Shem** (the name; or **Baruch Ha Shem**, blessed is the name)
8. **Shekinah** (Holy Spirit)
9. **El Eliyon** (the Most High God)
10. **Sh'Mah Yisrael Adonai Elohainu Adonai Chad** (Hear, O Israel, the Lord our God, the Lord is One.)
11. **Barukh Ata Adonai** (Blessed is the Lord)
12. **Kadoish, Kadoish, Kadoish, Adonai 'Tzebayoth** (Holy, holy, holy is the Lord God of Hosts)
13. **Eli Eli** (My God, my God)
14. **Ruach Elohim** (Spirit of the Godhead)
15. **Ribono Shel Olam** (Lord of the Universe)
16. **Shekinah Ruach Ha Quodesh** (Divine Presence of the Holy Spirit)

17. **Ain Sof Ur** (Limitless Light of the Absolute)
18. **Layoo-esh Shekinah** (Pillar of Light of the Holy Spirit)
19. **Ehyeh Metatron** (I Am Metatron; Metatron is an archangel who is the representative of God in the outer universe; often called the Garment of Shaddai, the visible manifestation of deity and creator of the outer worlds, creator of the electron)
20. **Yahweh Elohim** (Divine Lords of Light and Learning)
21. **Yeshua Michael** (Jesus and Archangel Michael)
22. **Shaddai El Chai** (the Almighty Living God)
23. **Adonai H'artez** (Lord of the Earth)
24. **Moshe, Yeshua, Eliahu** (Moses, Jesus and Elijah)
25. **Shalom** (Peace)
26. **Hyos Ha Koidesh** (Highest Servants of the Ancient of Days)

Hindu Mantras

1. **Aum or Om** (mother of all mantras)
2. **Brahma, Vishnu, Shiva** (the Hindu trinity: Creator, Preserver and Destroyer)
3. **So Ham** (I Am He, or I Am the Self, the mantra of Sai Baba and Baba Muktananda. It is the sound as God listens to the breath of humans. At night while humans sleep the sound becomes Aum, according to Sai Baba. When you breathe in, say *So*, when you breathe out, say *Ham*. Let the breath lead the meditation and mantra.)
4. **The Gayatri Mantra** (the holiest mantra of the Hindu religion, the equivalent of the Christian's The Lord's Prayer)

> *Bhur bhuvah svah,*
> *Tat-savitur varenyam*
> *Bhargo devasya dhimahi*
> *Dhiyo yo na pracodayat.*

Translation:

bhur(h)	Earth (body)
bhuvah	atmosphere (breath)
svah	heavens (cosmic mind)
tat-savituh(r)	of that source
varenyam	sacred (to be revered)
bhargo(gah)	light
devasya	effulgent, radiant
dhimahi	we meditate on
dhiyo(yal)	our thoughts
yo(yah)	which
na	our
pracodayat	should propel, urge, direct

Om Earth, atmosphere, heavens,
We meditate on the sacred light of that
effulgent source which should direct (be the
impulse for) our thoughts.

5. **Sai Baba or Sai Ram or Om Sri Sai Ram** (these will attract Sathya Sai Baba)
6. **Hare Krishna, Hare Krishna, Krishna, Krishna, Hare, Hare. Hare Rama, Hare Rama, Rama, Rama, Hare Hare.**
   (Hail to Krishna, Hail to Krishna, Krishna, Krishna, Hail, Hail. Hail to Rama, Hail to Rama, Rama, Rama, Hail, Hail. This is the Hare Krishna chant, used to disperse the negativity that covers our true nature.)
7. **Om Namah Shivaya** (This invokes the Supreme Guru who is the Self of all. This is the mantra of Baba Muktananda and Swami Sivananda.)
8. **Om Sri Dattatreya Namaha** (Om, honor the name of Dattatreya. Dattatreya is the incarnation of Brahma, Vishnu, and Shiva living in the same body. Sai Baba has said he is the incarnation of the Lord Dattatreya.)
9. **Om Shanti** (Mantra of Peace)
10. **Om Tat Sat** (Thou art the Inexpressible Absolute Reality)
11. **Hari Om Tat Sat** (Om, the Divine Absolute Reality)
12. **Hari Om** (a healing mantra; Hari is a name for Vishnu, the healing aspect of Lord Krishna)
13. **Om Sri Rama Jaya Rama Jaya Jaya Rama** (Victory for the Spiritual Self)
14. **Yesu Christu** (Jesus Christ, in Hindu)
15. **Rama** (a name of God, He who fills us with abiding joy)
16. **Krishna** (a name of God, He who draws us to Him)
17. **Tat Twam Asi** (That and This of One)
18. **Hong Sau** (I Am He, or I Am the Self. This mantra is done following the breath in the same manner as the So Ham and Ham Sa mantras. This was Paramahansa Yogananda's mantra.)
19. **Lam** (first chakra)
20. **Vam** (second chakra)
21. **Ram** (third chakra)
22. **Yam** (fourth chakra)
23. **Ham** (fifth chakra)
24. **Om** (sixth chakra)
25. **Aum** (seventh chakra)
26. **Sat Nam** (mantra of the Sikhs and of Guru Nanak)

27. **Eck Ong Kar Sat Nam Siri Wha Guru** ("The Supreme is One, His names are many")
28. **Sivo Ham** ("I Am Shiva")
29. **Aham Brahmasmi** ("I Am Brahman" or "I Am God")
30. **Om Ram Ramaya Namaha** ("O Lord Ram, I bow down to you")

Islamic Mantras

1. **Allahu Akbar** (God is Great)
2. **Bismillah Al-Rahman, Al-Rahim** (In the name of Allah, the Compassionate, the Merciful)
3. **Ya-Rahman** (God, the Beneficent)
4. **Ya-Salaam** (The Source of Peace)
5. **Ya-Mutakabir** (God, the Majestic)
6. **Ya-Ghaffar** (God, the Forgiver)
7. **Ya-Fattah** (God, the Opener)
8. **Ya-Hafiz** (God, the Preserver)
9. **Ya-Sabur** (God, the Patient)

Western Mantras

1. **I Am that I Am**
2. **I Am God**
3. **I Am**
4. **I Will**
5. **I Love**
6. **Be Still and Know I Am God**
7. **Areeeoooommm** (Edgar Cayce's mantra of Universal Mind)

Egyptian Mantras

1. **Nuk-Pu-Nuk** (I Am He I Am)
2. **Au-U Ur-Se-Ur Au-U** (I Am the Great One, Son of the Great One, I Am)
3. **Ra** (Egyptian sun god)
4. **Ra-Neter-Atef-Nefer** (the divine god, Ra, is gracious)
5. **Nefer-Neter-Wed-Neh** (the perfect God grants life)
6. **Osiris**
7. **Isis**
8. **Erta-Na-Hekau-Apen-Ast** (pronounced *err-tai no che-kah-oo o-pen ost*: May I be given the words of power of Isis)
9. **Heru-Udjat** (Eye of Horus)

Christian Mantras

1. **Jesus Christ** (one of the most powerful mantras you can possibly say)
2. **God, Christ, Holy Spirit**

3. The Lord's Prayer:
   Our Father, Who art in heaven, hallowed be thy name. Thy kingdom come, thy will be done on Earth as it is in heaven. Give us this day our daily bread, and forgive us our debts as we forgive our debtors. And lead us not into temptation, but deliver us from evil. For thine is the kingdom and the power and the glory forever. Amen
4. Ave Maria (Hail Mary)
5. Hail Mary, full of grace! The Lord is with thee. Blessed art thou amongst women, and blessed is the fruit of thy womb, Jesus. Holy Mary, Mother of God, pray for us sinners now and at the hour of our death.

Word Mantras

Peace, Joy, Love, Equilibrium, Personal Power, Forgiveness, Humility, Humbleness, Even-mindedness, Balance, Centeredness, Bliss, Compassion, Service, Goodwill, Altruism, Loving kindness, Oneness

The Tibetan Foundation Chakra Mantras

O   (first chakra)
Shu   (second chakra; pronounced shuck)
Ya   (third chakra)
Wa   (fourth chakra; pronounced yawn)
He   (fifth chakra)
Hu   (sixth chakra; pronounced hue)
I   (seventh chakra)

Buddhist Mantras

1. **Om Mani Padme Hum** (the Jewel [of compassion] in the Lotus [of the heart], one of the most powerful mantras in the world today)
2. **Om Ah Hum** (Come toward me, Om)
3. **Padme Siddhi Hum** (Come to me, O Lotus Power)
4. **Buddha**
5. **Quan Yin, Avalokitesvara, Chenrazee**

4

Structuring Your Classes

The core of each class is based on reading together certain chapters or sections from my books or other books you might choose, followed by a discussion. The second part of each class is more experiential and generally involves meditation. A third part, which follows both the reading session and the meditation, provides time for personal sharing, questions and answers and discussion.

Each class basically follows this format:

- Standard opening
- Reading aloud part of a chapter
- Sharing, questions and answers, discussion
- Break
- Experiential meditation (through audio tape or guided by leader)
- Sharing, more questions and answers, discussion
- Standard closing
- Social and networking time

The Opening

The basic structure of every class will begin first with the opening ceremony as described in chapter one. All invocations and prayers are done in unison.

1. Clearing Negative Energies: The Burning Pot
2. Unifying the Group Energy: Holding Hands
3. Establishing the Ascension Column and Pillar of Light
4. Clearing with the Platinum Net
5. Axiatonal Alignment
6. The Ascension Flame
7. Invoking the Spiritual and Cosmic Hierarchy
8. The Soul and Monad Mantras
9. Michael's Golden Dome of Protection
10. The Great Invocation
11. Three *Oms*
12. Optional Prayers

The Lesson

Next, read aloud one of the chapters from one of my books. I recommend that class members take turns as the book is passed around the room. (In a later chapter I will give you choices for class topics as brainstormed and channeled by myself and the ascended masters.) No one should feel obligated to read out loud. Some people do not like doing it, and this should be respected. Tell the group that if a person does not wish to read, just say "Pass." Keep this to 30 or 40 minutes. The length will depend on the total length of the class. If it is a two-hour class, 30 minutes is all the time you will have. If it is a two-and-a-half-hour class, you have time for 50 minutes. Since you will not likely have enough time to read an entire chapter, the leader of the group should pick out the sections of the chapter in advance that they feel will be the most beneficial. If any class members have questions or comments about the reading, encourage them to speak up. This phase of the class is specifically designed by the masters to stimulate the mental and intuitive bodies. Questions can be answered by the leader and/or class members. Discussion should be encouraged.

Then a 10-minute break should be taken to give everyone a chance to stretch and socialize.

The Meditation or Exercise

The third phase has been designed by the inner-plane ascended masters to be more experiential than the second, which was more didactic. This can be done in five ways: (1) Use one of my eight ascension meditation tapes. Each lasts about forty-five minutes. They are powerful meditations recorded in my voice, many during Wesak festivals.

(2) Lead the meditations yourself. I have enclosed the printed versions of these in this chapter.

(3) Have someone in the class who is proficient in voice channeling, channel the master who wants to speak on this subject. You and class members should ask questions to help stimulate the flow of information. If you don't have a proficient channeler, doing the meditations is quite effective and in some ways even better. It is also possible to do a combination of both.

(4) Occasionally have the class break up into groups of two or three for certain experiential exercises.

(5) You or possibly another class member can lead a meditation of choice. It is important for you to check out other class members' meditations in advance to make sure they are of high enough quality. The simplest path is to use the meditations I have provided in both audio and written form.

Sharing

When the meditation is complete, have a 10-minute period or longer for sharing experiences.

The Closing

When the sharing is completed, begin the closing ceremony. All invocations, prayers and *oms* are done in unison.

1. Clearing with the Platinum Net
2. Axiatonal Alignment
3. Removing the Core-Fear Matrix
4. Infusing Core Love and the Christ/Buddha Qualities
5. The Soul and Monad Mantras
6. Visiting the Golden Chamber of Melchizedek
    Group Prayer for Self and Others
    Prayers of Protection
    Prayer to Hold and Retain Energies
    Prayer for Ascension Acceleration
    Return and Grounding
7. Invoking a Golden Cylinder
8. Invoking Galactic Healers and Healing Angels
9. The Great Invocation
10. Three Oms
11. Prayer of Thanksgiving

Social and Networking Time and After

After everyone leaves, it is also a good idea, though not required, to light another burning pot in the center of the room where the class was held. With this curriculum there will be good, positive energy in your house because of the deep cleansing that takes place. Lighting another burning pot to reclaim your space is probably a good idea but is not mandatory.

I obviously recommend many chapters from my books because they are so easy to read, comprehensive and practical. However, if you feel guided to use other material, that is fine. Trust your own intuition and creativity. I am supplying a tentative plan given to me by the masters and my own God-self.

Each group will take on its own tone, unique focus and personality, depending on the leaders and class members. Do not be afraid to experiment. If you ever feel lost, you can always go back to the structure I have supplied. Feel free to build upon this structure or change it.

I have supplied audio-tape meditations and other meditations in written form that are some of the most powerful on the planet. Take advantage of them. However, if you have meditations of your own or those of other people or spiritual books or groups you've been involved with, feel free to work this material in. It is also possible to work in musical meditations and/or even silent meditations. Trust your inner guidance.

Structuring the class with some theoretical work and some experiential work is, I feel, a good balance. Too much meditation is not good and too much theoretical work is not good. Too much discussion and sharing is not good, either. Try to find a balance of these three.

Some other possibilities to spice up your classes is to invite an occasional guest speaker or guest channel and substitute that for a reading section. Another possibility is to have members of the group do occasional channelings. Still another possibility is to have group members share some of their spiritual and/or professional work. This could take the form, for example, of sharing something about the spiritual lineage or mystery school they are involved with. Other examples might be sharing work they do in magnified healing, Reiki, Bach flower remedies, psychological or spiritual training, spiritual art or music, to just name a few. The leader will need to decide how well this works or if it is something the group members want. These are extra things you can do, though the core of every class is the study of one of the chapters and an experiential meditation.

In most classes you will not have time to read a whole chapter, so it is the job of the leader to make selections from the chapter in advance, picking out the parts you feel are best for your group to take turns reading out loud. Make sure they know that if anyone has any comments, sharing or questions, they are free to stop the flow of the reading. In some class sessions you may read only a few pages and a discussion might take the rest of the time in that portion of the class. It is up to the leader to determine how the discussion is going and intervene when appropriate. Balance is the key.

Every class should have a meditation. Feel free to use the audio meditation tapes and the written meditations in this book over and over again. These meditations are so powerful and so packed full of activations, ideally they should be done almost every day for years on end to reap their full benefit. A meditation is different from reading a book, which you can read once or twice and won't need to read again. These meditations could be done a thousand times, yet you would still benefit enormously from the thousand-and-first time. This is because these are not only planetary ascension activations, they are also cosmic ascension activations. Realistically, living on Earth one could never garner the full potential of these meditations, for God is too infinite. It is their repetition over many years that bears the greatest fruit. An average meditation has one or two activations, but each meditation I have provided has hundreds of activations, not just planetary, but cosmic. You could truly never get your fill of cosmic ascension activations. To do so you would have to complete your 352 levels of initiation—an impossibility living on Earth. So, my beloved readers, use these meditations over and over again and experience the spiritual and energetic effects. I guarantee you that the experience will be so profound that it will feel like it is new every time.

My final suggestion, which I have not included in the official structure but that I highly recommend if you are at all comfortable doing it, is taking 15 to 20 minutes each session to sing bhajans, or devotional songs. I didn't put this in the structure of the class because some people are uncomfortable with it and may have no experience with it, which makes it hard to integrate comfortably. You might order from the Sai Baba bookstore in Tustin, CA (714) 669-0522, the bhajans in English on audio cassette. I myself love them and listen to them in my car whenever I drive. This might be a way to introduce them. Later, song sheets could be typed that give your favorite ones, then the class could sing along with the audio tapes. Sai Baba has said that singing devotional songs, or bhajans, is one of the best ways to clear negative ego from one's consciousness. If you are comfortable with this idea, you might consider it for your class even though I have not structured it into the sessions. Use your own intuition about it. You can always integrate it later once you have more experience doing the classes.

Practice experiencing and feeling the presence of each of the ascended masters and great beings of light as you progress through these classes. Through this practice you will come to know them in a more personal and profound manner. Each class has been structured to work with a different set of inner-plane ascended masters as well as to travel or bilocate to different inner-plane ashrams and ascension seats. Through these classes you will receive a well-rounded, synthesized education about some of the most well-known inner-plane ascended masters in the Planetary and Cosmic Hierarchy. You will also receive a broad experience and education in working with the different inner-plane ashrams and ascension seats. Do enjoy and become sensitized to the distinct subtle vibrations each class presents.

Once you do three or four of the classes you will see how easy it is to teach ascension classes. It takes just a little organization in the beginning, and then you will see that every class is organized the same way, but with a different content. So enjoy yourself and have fun!

5

Ascension-Activation Meditations

Personal Growth Meditations

1 Cosmic-Ray Meditation

Close eyes. Let us begin by having everyone take a deep breath. Exhale.

We call all the masters of the Planetary and Cosmic Hierarchy to help in this meditation.

We call forth a planetary and cosmic axiatonal alignment.

We call to Melchizedek, Mahatma and Metatron for the anchoring of the Platinum Net to clear away any and all unwanted energies.

We call on Archangel Michael to establish a dome of protection for this session.

We call forth the establishment now of a pillar of light and a planetary and cosmic ascension column for this session.

We now begin the process of fully anchoring and activating the planetary and cosmic rays.

We begin by calling forth the ascended master El Morya, the chohan of the first ray, to now fully anchor and activate the first ray, representing the Will of God, which is red in color.

Bathe in the positive effects of this red ray now.

We now call forth Master Kuthumi and the ascended master Djwhal Khul to now fully anchor and activate the second ray of Love/Wisdom, which is blue in color.

Bathe in the positive effects of this blue ray now.

We now call forth Master Serapis Bey, who is the chohan of the third ray, to now fully anchor and activate the third ray of Active Intelligence, which is yellow in color.

Bathe in the positive effects of this yellow ray now.

We now call forth Master Paul the Venetian, who is the chohan of the fourth ray, to now fully anchor and activate the fourth ray of Harmony, which is emerald green in color.

Bathe in the positive effects of this emerald-green ray now.

We now call forth Master Hilarion, who is the chohan of the fifth ray, to now fully anchor and activate the fifth ray of New Age Science, which is orange in color.

Bathe in the positive effects of this orange ray now.

We now call forth Sananda, the chohan of the sixth ray, who in one of his past lives was known as the Master Jesus, to now fully anchor and activate the sixth ray of Devotion, which is indigo in color.

Bathe in the positive effects of this indigo ray now.

We now call forth Saint Germain, the chohan of the seventh ray, who has recently taken over the position in the spiritual government known as the Mahachohan. We now request the full anchoring and activation of the seventh ray of Ceremonial Order and Magic, which is violet in color.

Bathe now in the positive effects of this violet transmuting flame.

We now call forth the seven ray masters and Master Djwhal Khul to clear all lower and/or negative attributes from these first seven rays, and replace them with the higher and positive attributes of the Christ/Buddha archetype and imprint.

We now call forth the Master Lady Nada to fully anchor and activate the eighth ray of Higher Cleansing, which is sea-foam green in color.

Bathe in the positive effects of this sea-foam green ray now.

We now call forth the Virgin Mary to fully anchor and activate the ninth ray of Joy and Attracting the Lightbody, which is blue-green in color.

Bathe in the positive effects of this blue-green ray now.

We now call forth Allah Gobi, who holds the position in the spiritual government known as the Manu, which is a higher governmental position of the first ray. He has volunteered this evening to officially activate the tenth ray, which has to do with fully anchoring the lightbody, and this ray is pearlescent in color.

Bathe in the positive effects of this pearlescent ray now.

We now call forth Quan Yin, the bodhisattva of compassion, to now fully anchor and activate the eleventh ray, which serves as a bridge to the new age, and is pink/orange in color.

Bathe in the positive effects of this pink/orange ray now.

We now call forth the Lady Master Pallas Athena to now fully anchor and activate the twelfth ray, which embodies the full anchoring of the new age and the Christ consciousness, which is gold in color.

Bathe in the positive effects of this gold ray now.

We now move from the planetary rays to the cosmic rays.

We now call forth Lord Buddha, our new Planetary Logos, to fully anchor and activate the Shamballic ray of pure white light.

Bathe in the profundity and glory of this pure white light from Lord Buddha himself.

We call forth Helios and Vesta, our Solar Logos, to now fully anchor and activate the cosmic solar ray from the solar core, which is copper-gold in color.

Bathe in the wonderful positive effects of this copper-gold cosmic ray now.

We now call forth Melchior, our Galactic Logos, to fully anchor and activate the galactic ray, which is silver-gold in color.

Bathe and soak in this exquisite silver/gold ray.

We now call forth Lord Melchizedek, our Universal Logos, for the full anchoring and activation of the universal ray, which is the purest and most refined golden vibration available to Earth.

Bathe and absorb into every cell of your being this golden radiation from Melchizedek.

We now call forth Archangel Metatron to fully anchor and activate the ten lost cosmic rays of the Yod spectrum, which are all hues of platinum.

Bathe now and fully absorb these ten lost cosmic platinum hues.

We now call forth the Multiuniversal Logos to now fully anchor and activate the core platinum ray.

Become like a sponge and soak in this core platinum ray.

We now call forth the Mahatma, is a cosmic group consciousness embodying all 352 levels of the Godhead, to now fully anchor and activate the Mahatma ray, which is a cosmic white light containing all colors of the spectrum.

Soak in this rainbow-colored light, taking it into the essence of your being.

We now call to the Cosmic Council of Twelve, who are the twelve cosmic beings that surround the Throne of Grace to fully anchor and activate their twelve cosmic rays, which are so refined that they are translucent and beyond all color.

Let these exquisite rays and translucent vibrations soak into the essence of your heart and soul.

Last, we call forth the presence of God and request an anchoring and activation of the clear light of the ray of God.

Let us enter the silence now . . .

Let us now come back into our bodies, continuing to absorb and enjoy these refined cosmic rays.

2 Meditation in the Golden Chamber of Melchizedek

Close your eyes and take a deep breath. Exhale.

We call all the masters of the Planetary and Cosmic Hierarchy to help in this meditation.

We now call forth a planetary and cosmic axiatonal alignment.

This meditation will set in place all the spiritual hookups needed to fully activate all present to their highest ascension potentiality.

Allow yourself to completely relax and soak in all the cosmic energies and ascension activations.

We now call to the seven chohans, Djwhal Khul, Lord Maitreya and Lord Buddha to provide a gigantic group merkabah. We ask to be taken spiritually to the Golden Chamber of Melchizedek in the universal core.

We call forth each person's 144 soul extensions from their monad and mighty I Am Presence to join us if they choose for this meditation.

We call to the seven chohans for the opening of all chakras, the ascension chakra and all petals and facets of all chakras.

We call to Archangel Metatron for the permanent anchoring and activation of the microtron.

We call to the Lord of Sirius for the anchoring and activation of the scrolls of wisdom and knowledge appropriate for this group from the Great White Lodge on Sirius.

We also ask to be connected to the cosmic initiation that Vywamus has recently taken for the purpose of accelerated ascension activation.

We call to Sanat Kumara, Vywamus and Lenduce for help in establishing each person's planetary and cosmic antakarana that connects each person's oversoul and monad to God.

We call to Melchizedek, Mahatma, Metatron, the Elohim Councils and the archangels for the permanent anchoring and activation of the planetary and cosmic Tree of Life.

We request the complete opening and activation of the Seven Cosmic Seals and the Ten Sephiroth, as well as the hidden sephiroth of Daath.

We call forth from the Cosmic and Planetary Hierarchy the anchoring and activation of all fire letters, key codes and sacred geometries to help in this process.

We call to the archangels for the full anchoring and activation of our 50 chakras, taking us through planetary ascension as well as our 330 chakras, taking us back to the Godhead.

We call for the permanent anchoring and activation of our twelve bodies, including the solar, galactic and universal bodies.

We call to Melchizedek, the Mahatma, Metatron, Archangel Michael and the Planetary Hierarchy for the anchoring and activation of the anointed Christ overself body, our zohar body, our overself body, our electromagnetic body, our gematrian body, our eka body, our epi-kinetic body, our higher Adam Kadmon body and the Lord's mystical body as described in The Keys of Enoch.

We call forth the permanent anchoring and activation of the 64 keys of Enoch in all five sacred languages.

We call forth the illumination of the 72 areas of the mind, as described in The Keys of Enoch.

We call forth the deca-delta light encodements and emanations from the ten superscripts of the divine Mind.

We call to Metatron for the anchoring and activation of the 76 names of Metatron to permanently flow through us.

We call for the removal of all veils of light and time.

We call to Djwhal Khul, Lord Maitreya and Lord Buddha for the permanent anchoring of the Greater Flame of the monad and mighty I Am Presence, into the Lesser Flame of the personality and soul incarnated on Earth.

We call to the mighty archangels for the permanent anchoring and activation of the twelve heavenly houses and twelve cosmic stations.

We call to Lord Buddha for the permanent anchoring and activation of the planetary Sun and the planetary Cosmic Heart into the core of our being.

We call to Helios and Vesta for the permanent anchoring and activation of the solar Sun and the solar Cosmic Heart into the core of our being.

We call to Melchior for the permanent anchoring and activation of the galactic Sun and galactic Cosmic Heart into the core of our being.

We call to Melchizedek for the permanent anchoring and activation of the universal Sun and universal Cosmic Heart into the core of our being.

We call to the Mahatma and the Multiuniversal Logos to permanently anchor and activate the multiuniversal Sun and multiuniversal Cosmic Heart into the core of our being.

We call to the Godhead for the permanent anchoring and activation of the Great Central Sun and God's Heart into the core of our being.

We call to the Source of our cosmic day and Melchizedek for the anchoring of the 43 christed universes.

We call to Melchizedek to initiate each person present into the Order of Melchizedek.

We ask that each person who inwardly gives permission, now receives from Melchizedek the rod of initiation, with no earthly person needed as an intermediary in this process.

We call to the Planetary and Cosmic Hierarchy and collectively request a complete merger of the lightbodies of all the inner-plane masters present with this group body, both individually and collectively.

We call forth God, the Mahatma, Melchizedek, Metatron, Elohim Councils, Archangel Michael and the other archangels to anchor from the cosmic Treasury of Light, the light packets of information from the Tablets of Creation, the Elohim Scriptures, the Torah Or, the Ten Commandments and the cosmic

Book of Life.

We now call to the Planetary and Cosmic Hierarchy and all the inner-plane masters that accompany each person for a combined light shower, the likes of which this world has never known before.

Let us close by repeating together the famous mantra from The Keys of Enoch:

Kodoish, Kodoish, Kodoish, Adonai 'Tsebayoth: Holy, Holy, Holy is the Lord God of Hosts!

We now call forth our inner-plane spiritual hosts and request to be taken together in our group merkabah back into our physical bodies into this room.

3 Specialized Ascension Activations

Close your eyes. Let us begin by taking a deep breath. Exhale.

We call forth all the masters from the Planetary and Cosmic Hierarchy to help in this meditation.

We now call for a planetary and cosmic axiatonal alignment.

We call forth Melchizedek, the Mahatma and Metatron to anchor the Platinum Net to clear away any and all unwanted energies.

We call forth Lord Buddha, our Planetary Logos, and request the permanent anchoring and activation of all God crystals and seed packets from Shamballa.

We now move up to the solar level and call forth Helios and Vesta to anchor and activate all the God crystals and seed packets from the solar core.

We now move to the galactic level and call forth Melchior to anchor and activate all the God crystals and seed packets from the galactic core.

We now move up to the universal level and call forth Melchizedek to anchor and activate all the God crystals and seed packets from the universal core.

We now move to the multiuniversal level and call forth the Multiuniversal Logos to anchor and activate all the God crystals and seed packets from the multiuniversal core.

We now move to the 352d level of the Godhead and call directly to God, the Cosmic Council of Twelve, and the Twenty-Four

Elders that surround the Throne of Grace to anchor and activate all the God crystals and seed packets from the Heart of God.

As we continue to absorb the God crystals, seed packets and cosmic energies from Source, the Mahatma energy asks if you are willing to be a planetary anchor and focus for its cosmic energies. If you are willing, inwardly give your consent to the Mahatma within the core of your being.

For those who have agreed, we will now take 30 seconds of silence while the Mahatma energy runs through us, embodying all 352 levels of God.

We now call forth from the Mahatma energy the opening of the 352 levels of the heart, in a holographic penetration of the Mahatma's entire being.

We now call forth from Melchizedek, Metatron, the Mahatma, archangels and the Elohim Councils to anchor and active all fire letters, key codes, sacred geometries and the master divine blueprint for each person present.

We now call forth to our inner-plane spiritual hosts for the anchoring and activation of the light grid of ascension for all monads of the 144,000 currently working on ascension.

We now call forth the beloved master Kuthumi, the chohan of the second ray, who will now bestow the status of World Teacher to all who are in attendance at this time, if you choose to receive this blessing.

Visualize yourself now standing before Master Kuthumi, with your palms held open and turned upward, and see him first touching your heart, then your third eye, then your crown chakra.

Feel the spiritual current run through you as you now take on this mantle of responsibility.

We now call forth the divine Mother, Quan Yin, Vesta, Lakshmi, Lady of the Sun, Lady Liberty, Portia, Lady Nada, Pallas Athena, Lady of the Light, Lady Helena, Hilda, Alice Bailey, Isis, the Virgin Mary and all the lady masters of the Planetary and Cosmic Hierarchy.

We call forth from this great Sisterhood of Light the full anchoring and activation of the divine feminine within, in order that it resonate in perfect harmony to the divine masculine within.

We ask for a complete balancing of the male/female, yin/yang energies within each of our selves so that these energies may flow and manifest in perfect harmony and ease as God would have it be.

Visualize now the divine Mother placing a lotus blossom composed of the love/wisdom and power of God within the center of each person's heart.

We also now request that the divine Mother and lady masters become permanently anchored inside our hearts.

We now call forth Archangel Metatron and request a divine dispensation for the full anchoring and activation of the Platinum Rod for each person in attendance who wishes to receive this grace and blessing.

We call forth the ascended master Djwhal Khul from the Planetary Synthesis Ashram to officially anchor and activate, with the help of the seven chohans, each person's divine puzzle piece so that all present may easily and effortlessly fulfill their divine mission and life's purpose.

We call forth El Morya, Kuthumi, Djwhal Khul, Serapis Bey, Paul the Venetian, Hilarion, Sananda, Saint Germain, Allah Gobi, Lord Maitreya, Lord Buddha and Vywamus for help in weaving each person's ascension fabric for rising to the next level of planetary and cosmic ascension realization.

We now call forth Melchizedek, the Mahatma, Metatron, Lord Michael, the archangels and the Elohim Councils for light-quotient building at the highest potential available to each person individually and to the entire group body.

We now call forth the divine Mother, Helios and Vesta, Quan Yin, Lord Maitreya and the Virgin Mary for love-quotient building at the highest potential available to each person and to the entire group body.

4 God Ascension Seat Meditation

Close your eyes. Let us begin by taking a deep breath. Exhale.

We call forth all the masters of the Planetary and Cosmic Hierarchy to help in this meditation.

We call for a planetary and cosmic axiatonal alignment.

We call to our inner-plane spiritual hosts to completely balance the energies in this room.

We call Melchizedek, the Mahatma and Metatron to anchor the Platinum Net to clear away any and all unwanted energies.

We now call forth our inner-plane spiritual hosts to provide a group merkabah, like a gigantic boat, for everyone present.

We ask to be taken in this merkabah to Shamballa to sit in the ascension seat of Lord Buddha, our Planetary Logos.

Feel and absorb the energies of this planetary ascension seat.

We call forth from Lord Buddha a special divine dispensation of ascension activation for this group.

As a final blessing from Lord Buddha, we request a divine dispensation to experience the Light Rod of Lord Buddha, which will ignite our ascension realization even further.

Let us receive this special blessing now.

We now call to our inner-plane spiritual hosts to move our gigantic group merkabah from the planetary to the solar level to visit Helios and Vesta and sit in their solar ascension seat.

Feel and sense the difference between the ascension seat in Shamballa and the ascension seat of Helios and Vesta in the solar core.

Feel and absorb these energies.

We call forth from Helios and Vesta the most accelerated ascension activation available to us at this time.

We also now call forth a special divine dispensation to experience the Light Rod of Helios and Vesta, which will ignite and catalyze our ascension growth even further.

Let us receive this special blessing now.

We now call forth our inner-plane spiritual hosts and ask to be taken in our group merkabah to the galactic core, and the ascension seat of Melchior, our Galactic Logos.

Feel the difference in frequency between the solar ascension seat and the galactic ascension seat you are now sitting in.

We now call forth the merging of three other galactic ascension seats with the one we are currently sitting in. We call forth the ascension seats of the Lord of Sirius, Lenduce and the Lord of Arcturus to blend together so we may experience the effects of combining them.

We now request from Melchior, the Lord of Sirius, Lenduce and the Lord of Arcturus the greatest possible ascension acceleration available to us now.

We now call for a special divine dispensation to experience the combined Light Rods of these four great and noble masters.

Let us now receive this unique and special blessing.

We now call forth our inner-plane spiritual hosts and ask to be taken in our group merkabah to the Golden Chamber of

Melchizedek at the universal level to sit in his ascension seat.

Notice again the difference in frequency and quality of energy between the galactic ascension seat and the universal ascension seat you are now sitting in.

We also call forth while at this universal level a special divine dispensation from the archangels, Michael/Faith, Jophiel/Christine, Chamuel/Charity, Gabriel/Hope, Raphael/Mother Mary, Uriel/Aurora, Zadkiel/Amethyst, the seven mighty elohim and their divine counterparts, an ascension acceleration for each person and the group body.

We now call forth from Lord Melchizedek the greatest possible ascension acceleration available to us at this time.

We now call forth from Melchizedek a special divine dispensation to experience his Light Rod.

Let us receive this very special blessing and grace now.

We now ask Melchizedek to take us in our group merkabah to the next level, which is the multiuniversal level, to sit in the multiuniversal ascension seat by the grace of the Mahatma and the Multiuniversal Logos.

Feel an even more refined frequency at this rarefied vibration.

We call to the Mahatma and the Multiuniversal Logos for a divine dispensation for the greatest possible ascension acceleration available to us at this time.

We now call for the Mahatma and the Multiuniversal Logos to take the group merkabah up to the next level, which is the ascension seat of the divine Mother at the left hand of God.

Feel the sublime energies of this ascension seat.

We call forth to the divine Mother for a divine dispensation of the greatest possible ascension acceleration available to us individually and collectively at this time.

Bathe in the divine cosmic love and acceleration of the divine Mother at this 352d level of divinity.

We call forth to the divine Mother and ask that our group merkabah now be taken to the ascension seat of the divine Father at the right hand of God.

Bathe now in these most exquisite and sublime energies of the divine Father's ascension seat.

We call forth to the divine Father for a divine dispensation of the greatest possible ascension acceleration available to each of us individually and collectively at this time.

Absorb this divine Father acceleration into the core and essence of your being.

Last, we call forth the divine Mother, the divine Father, the Mahatma, Melchizedek, Metatron and Lord Michael to now take us in our group merkabah to the Throne of Grace to sit in God's ascension seat.

Let us humbly receive this blessing now, as we enter into the silence.

From the bottom of our hearts we thank the beloved presence of God for this most sanctified blessing and grace.

We now call forth the divine Mother, the divine Father, the Mahatma, Melchizedek, Metatron and Lord Michael and humbly request to be taken in our group merkabah back down through all the levels and dimensions of reality into our physical bodies.

5 Fifty-Point Cosmic Cleansing Meditation

Close your eyes. Let us begin by all taking a deep breath. Exhale.

The meditation we are about to do is quite deep. It will foster an enormous ascension acceleration, so completely relax and be like a sponge, letting the masters do their divine handiwork.

We call forth the entire Planetary and Cosmic Hierarchy for help in implementing this meditation for the entire group.

We call forth a planetary and cosmic axiatonal alignment.

We call forth Lord Michael to establish a golden dome of protection for all present.

We call to Vywamus and the archangels to bring forth their golden hands as a net to cleanse all negative energies in our energy field individually and collectively.

We call from Melchizedek, the Mahatma and Metatron the anchoring of the Platinum Net to cleanse the energy fields of each person even more deeply.

We now call forth to the Lord of Arcturus and the Arcturians for the anchoring of the prana wind clearing device both individually and in our group body.

See this prana wind clearing device as a fan anchored at the solar plexus, blowing and clearing all unwanted energies out of the etheric body.

Feel the prana wind clearing device now being lifted out of your field by the Lord of Arcturus and the beloved Arcturians.

We now call forth from Djwhal Khul, the seven chohans, Lord Maitreya, Allah Gobi, Lord Buddha and the cosmic masters to anchor the core-fear removal program.

See this as a latticework of light anchored into the four-body system, highlighting any negative energies or blockages in your energy fields.

We now call for the removal of all fear programming and blocks from every person in this room so they may achieve their ascension at the highest possible level.

See this fear programming as black roots intertwined in your energy fields, now being pulled out like a vacuum cleaner through your crown chakra by the masters.

Planetary and Cosmic Hierarchy, please now remove all separative thinking from the four-body system.

Please also now remove all judgmental programming from the four-body system.

Please remove all lack of forgiveness from the four-body system.

Feel these negative aspects again being pulled out of your energy fields and through the crown chakra like unwanted weeds being removed from a beautiful garden.

Planetary and Cosmic Hierarchy, please remove all impatience and negative anger.

Please remove all negative selfishness, self-centeredness and narcissism.

Please remove any negative thought forms, feelings and emotions and imbalanced archetypes from the four-body system.

Please remove all superiority and inferiority thinking created by the negative ego.

Please remove all aspects of guilt and shame consciousness created by the negative ego.

Please remove all negative-ego and fear-based programming in a generalized sense.

Please cleanse and remove all harmful extraterrestrial implants and negative elementals.

We call forth the cleansing and removal of all unwanted astral entities.

We call to Melchizedek, the Mahatma and Metatron for the cosmic viral vacuum to remove any clinical or subclinical viruses currently existing in any of our energy fields.

Please also remove all negative bacteria with the cosmic bacterial vacuum program.

We call to the archangels and the elohim to remove all disease energy from the physical, etheric, astral and mental vehicles.

We call forth each person's personal inner-plane healing angels to now heal and repair any irritations, spots and/or leaks in the aura.

We call forth to Melchizedek, the Mahatma, Metatron, Archangel Michael and the archangels for the removal of all improper soul fragments.

We also ask for the retrieval of all the soul fragments from the universe that belong to us in divine order.

We call forth each person's etheric healing team, and we now request that the etheric body be repaired and brought back to its perfect blueprint.

We call forth the anchoring now of each person's perfect divine monadic blueprint body and/or mayavarupa body, to be used from this moment forward to accelerate healing and spiritual growth on all levels during the rest of this lifetime.

We call forth a complete cleansing and clearing of our genetic line and ancestral lineage.

We call forth the Lord of Arcturus to now bring forth the golden cylinder to remove and vacuum up any and all remaining negative energy in our collective energy fields.

We call forth a clearing and cleansing of all past lives and future lives.

We call forth now the integration and cleansing of our 144 soul extensions from our monad and mighty I Am Presence.

We now call forth a clearing and cleansing of all karma.

(As you know, we need to balance 51 percent of our karma to take the beginning phase of our planetary ascension.)

We ask for the greatest possible cleansing of our karma now.

We call forth Melchizedek, Mahatma and Metatron to anchor a matchstick worth of cosmic fire to very gently burn away all astral, mental and etheric dross and gray clouds from our fields.

We now request a complete clearing and cleansing of our entire monad and mighty I Am Presence itself.

We now call forth the greatest cleansing process ever known from Melchizedek, Mahatma, Metatron, Lord Michael, the arch-angels, the Elohim Councils and from God.

We now call forth the ultimate cosmic cleansing and clearing all the way back to our original covenant with God at our original spiritual creation.

We will take a few moments of silence to receive this blessing and grace.

We now call forth from all the cosmic and planetary masters gathered here a downpouring and light shower of core love and the Christ/Buddha/Melchizedek attributes to replace all that has been removed and cleansed, by the grace of God and the Cosmic and Planetary Hierarchy.

We call on Archangel Sandalphon, Pan and the Earth Mother to help us become properly integrated and grounded back into our physical bodies.

We call forth our personal inner-plane healing angels to per-fectly balance our chakras and four-body system.

When you are ready, open your eyes and enjoy the sense of well-being and crystal clarity in your energy fields.

6 Ascension Meditation and Treatment

O, beloved God, Christ, Holy Spirit, mighty I Am Presence, my monad, I Am That I Am, Mahatma (Avatar of Synthesis), Seven Mighty Elohim, Melchior, our Galactic Logos, Ashtar Com-mand, archangels Michael, Jophiel, Chamuel, Gabriel, Raphael, Uriel, Zadkiel and Metatron, Helios (our Solar Logos), Sanat Kumara (our Planetary Logos), Lord Maitreya (the planetary Christ), Allah Gobi (the Manu), the Mahachohan, Sathya Sai Baba, beloved chohans of the seven rays—El Morya, Kuthumi, Serapis Bey, Paul the Venetian, Hilarion, Master Je-sus and Saint Germain—Lords of Karma, Djwhal Khul, Bud-dha, Vywamus, Virgin Mary, Quan Yin, Isis, Babaji, the Great Divine Director, Enoch, the Great White Brotherhood Medical Assistance Healing Team (Pan, Overlighting Angel of Healing, ascended masters and monad), Order of Melchizedek, Spiritual Hierarchy, Great White Brotherhood, Masters of Shamballa!

Beloved God and Mahatma, I choose now to accept and invoke a deep penetration of the Mahatma energy into my entire energy matrix, thereby allowing a full, open radiation of my divine self in service to All That Is.

We call forth from God and the God force a series of golden balls of light.

Feel these large golden balls of light coming down from God and your mighty I Am Presence, moving down your chakra column and entering your seven chakras.

Let the golden ball of light enter your first chakra.

I now fully open and activate my first chakra. I Am That I Am. Aum!

Let the golden ball enter your second chakra.

I now fully open and activate my second chakra. I Am That I Am. Aum!

I now fully open and activate my third chakra. I Am That I Am. Aum!

I now fully open and activate my fourth chakra. I Am That I Am. Aum!

I now fully open and activate my fifth chakra. I Am That I Am. Aum!

I now fully open and activate my sixth chakra. I Am That I Am. Aum!

I now fully open and activate my seventh chakra. I Am That I Am. Aum!

We now call forth our mighty I Am Presence, Archangel Michael and the Great White Brotherhood Medical Assistance Program (MAP) team (composed of Pan, ascended master healers, angels of healing and our own monad) to enter each chakra and per-fectly balance and attune it, removing any unwanted energies or cords of energy that are not for our highest God purpose and of our true divine monadic blueprint.

Take about fifteen seconds or more after each chakra invocation for its full cleansing, healing and balancing.

We now request the perfect integration and balancing of our chakras so they function as one unified chakra.

We now call forth the violet flame of Saint Germain to bathe our entire being in his violet transmuting flame. Let this beautiful violet energy flowing down from God transmute any and all negativity into the purity and perfection of God.

Bathe in this energy for about fifteen to thirty seconds.

We now call forth the golden twelfth ray and allow it to bathe our entire being in the energy of the Christ consciousness.

See your entire being and all seven bodies being filled with this luminous golden energy pouring down from God, your mighty I Am Presence and the ascended masters. Bathe in this twelfth-ray golden light for another 15 to 30 seconds.

We now request God and the God force to be placed within our living-light merkabah vehicle.

See the merkabah vehicle as a vertical double-terminated crystal that surrounds your entire body, with a similar but horizontal crystal projecting through the center of the vertical arm of this crystal cross. The merkabah will help accelerate and quicken your overall vibrational frequencies. It is also a vehicle in which you can soul-travel during meditation or during sleep.

Place yourself within the merkabah and allow it to spin clockwise. This spinning attunes you even more to the cosmic pulse and frequencies of God and the God force.

I am now ready for the ascension process to begin. *(The ascending process is really the descending process of spirit into matter.)* **Beloved God and God force, I now call forth my soul to fully descend into my consciousness and four-body system. I Am That I Am. Aum!**

I call forth my glorified lightbody to now descend into my consciousness and four-body system. I Am That I Am. Aum!

I call forth the ascension flame to descend and enter my consciousness and entire four-body system. I Am That I Am. Aum!

I call forth the full activation of my alpha and omega chakras. I Am That I Am. Aum! I call forth the Amrita, fire letters, sacred geometries and key codes from The Keys of Enoch **to now become fully activated. I Am that I Am. Aum!**

I now call forth the full activation and creation of the twelve strands of DNA within my physical vehicle. I Am That I Am. Aum!

I now call forth the full activation of my pituitary gland to create only the life hormone and stop producing the death hormone. I Am That I Am. Aum!

I now call forth and fully activate my monadic divine blueprints in my conscious, subconscious and superconscious minds and four-body system. I Am That I Am. Aum!

I now call forth and fully activate my kundalini energy as guided by my monad and mighty I Am Presence. I Am That I Am. Aum!

I now call forth a matchstick-sized spark of cosmic fire from the

presence of God Himself to illuminate and transform my entire being into the light of God. I Am That I Am. Aum!

I now call forth a full axiatonal alignment as described in The Keys of Enoch *to perfectly align all my meridian flows within my consciousness and four-body system. I Am That I Am. Aum!*

I now call forth and fully claim my physical immortality and the complete cessation of the aging and death process. I am now youthing and becoming younger every day. I Am That I Am. Aum!

I now call forth the full opening of my third eye and all my psychic and channeling abilities so that I may use them in the glory and service of God and my brothers and sisters in Christ on Earth. I Am That I Am. Aum!

I now call forth perfect, radiant health to manifest within my physical, emotional, mental, etheric and spiritual bodies. I ask and command that these bodies now manifest the health and perfection of Christ. I Am That I Am. Aum!

I now call forth my sixteenth chakra to descend, moving all my chakras down my chakra column until my sixteenth chakra resides in my seventh, or crown chakra. I Am That I Am. Aum!

I now call forth my fifteenth chakra to descend and enter my sixth, or third-eye chakra. I Am That I Am. Aum!

I now call forth my fourteenth chakra to descend and enter my throat chakra. I Am That I Am. Aum!

I now call forth my thirteenth chakra to descend, enter and reside in my heart chakra. I Am That I Am. Aum!

I now call forth my twelfth chakra to descend, enter and reside in my solar plexus chakra. I Am That I Am. Aum!

I now call forth my eleventh chakra to descend, enter and reside in my second chakra. I Am That I Am. Aum!

I now call forth my tenth chakra to descend, enter and reside in my first chakra. I Am That I Am. Aum!

I now see the rest of my chakras, nine through one, descend down my legs and into the Earth in a corresponding fashion. I Am That I Am. Aum!

I now call forth the complete stabilization of my new fifth-dimensional chakra grid system within my consciousness and four-body system. I Am That I Am. Aum!

I now call forth and see my chakra column lighting up like a Christmas tree with my first chakra becoming a large ball of pearl-white light.

My second chakra now becomes a large ball of pink-orange light.

My third chakra now becomes a glowing ball of golden light.

My heart chakra now lights up with a pale violet-pink light.

My fifth chakra now lights up with a deep blue-violet light.

My third-eye chakra now lights up with a large ball of golden white light.

My crown chakra now lights up with violet-white light.

My entire chakra column has now been ignited with the fifth-dimensional ascension frequency. I Am That I Am. Aum!

I now call forth with all my heart and soul and mind and might the collective help of my eleven other soul extensions in my ascension process. I Am That I Am. Aum!

I now call forth the combined collective help of the 143 other soul extensions of my monadic group in my ascension process. I Am That I Am. Aum!

I now call forth the complete descending and integration into my being of the raincloud of knowable things. I Am That I Am. Aum!

I now call forth the trinity of Isis, Osiris and Horus and all pyramid energies that are aligned with Source to now descend into my consciousness and four-body system and become fully activated now. I Am That I Am. Aum!

I also call forth the ascended master Serapis Bey and his Ascension Temple energies from Luxor to descend and become fully activated within my consciousness and four-body system now. I Am That I Am. Aum!

I now call forth an ascension column of light to surround my entire being. I Am That I Am. Aum!

I now call forth the complete balancing of all my karma from all my past and future lives. I Am That I Am. Aum!

I now call forth the raising of my vibrational frequencies within my physical, astral, mental, etheric and spiritual bodies to the fifth-dimensional frequencies. I Am That I Am. Aum!

I now call forth the light of a thousand suns to descend into my being and raise my vibrational frequencies one-thousandfold. I Am That I Am. Aum!

I now call forth the sacred sound of Aum to descend and reverberate through my consciousness and four-body system. I Am That I Am. Aum!

I now call forth a complete and full baptism of the Holy Spirit. I Am That I Am. Aum!

I now call forth the perfect attunement and completion of my dharma, purpose and mission in this lifetime in service of God's plan. I Am that I Am. Aum!

I call forth my fifth-dimensional ascended self, who is already ascended within the understanding of simultaneous time, to now meld its consciousness with my unified field and aura. I Am That I Am. Aum!

I call forth my spiritual teacher, [insert name], to descend through my crown chakra and meld his or her ascended consciousness and light into my consciousness and four-body system. I Am That I Am. Aum!

I call forth my monad, my mighty I Am Presence and spirit to now fully descend into my consciousness and four-body system and transform me into light and the ascended master I truly am. I Am That I Am. Aum!

Take a few minutes of silence to allow the complete ascension to fully take place while remaining on Earth. Upon complete merging with the light in consciousness and in your four-body system, recite the following affirmations of truth:

Be still and know I Am God. I Am That I Am. Aum!

I Am the resurrection and the life. I Am That I Am. Aum!

I Am the mighty I Am Presence on Earth forevermore. I Am That I Am. Aum!

I Am the ascended master [insert your full name]! I Am That I Am. Aum!

The mighty I Am Presence is now my real self. I Am That I Am. Aum!

I Am the ascension in the light. I Am That I Am. Aum!

I Am the truth, the way, and the light! I Am That I Am. Aum!

I Am the open door which no man can shut. I Am That I Am. Aum!

I Am divine perfection made manifest now. I Am That I Am. Aum!

I Am the revelation of God. I Am That I Am. Aum!

I Am the light that lights every soul that cometh into the world. I Am That I Am. Aum!

I Am the cosmic flame of cosmic victory. I Am That I Am. Aum!

I Am the ascended being I wish to be now. I Am That I Am. Aum!

I Am the raised vibration of my full Christ and I Am potential. I Am That I Am. Aum!

I Am the Aum made manifest in the world. I Am That I Am. Aum!

I Am a full member of the Great White Brotherhood and Spiritual Hierarchy. I Am That I Am. Aum!

I Am the realized manifestation of the eternal self. I Am That I Am. Aum!

I Am the embodiment of divine love in action. I Am That I Am. Aum!

I live within all beings and all beings live within me. I Am That I Am. Aum!

I Am now one with the monadic plane of consciousness on Earth! I Am That I Am. Aum!

I Am now living in my glorified body of light on Earth. I Am That I Am. Aum!

I now affirm my ability to transform my four bodies into light and travel anywhere in God's infinite universe. I Am That I Am. Aum!

I call forth to Helios, the Solar Logos, to now send forth into my consciousness through my crown chakra, the 64 keys of Enoch in all five sacred languages so they are fully integrated into my being on Earth. I Am That I Am. Aum!

I fully affirm my identity as the Eternal Self, the Christ, the Buddha, the atma, the monad, the I Am Presence on Earth in service of humankind. I Am That I Am. Aum!

I fully affirm that I Am physically immortal and I can, if I choose, remain on Earth indefinitely without aging. I Am That I Am. Aum!

I see every person, animal and plant as the embodiment of the Eternal Self, whether they are aware of their true identity or not. I Am That I Am. Aum!

I Am now the perfect integration of the monad, soul and person-
ality on Earth. I Am That I Am. Aum!

In this holy instant has salvation come. I Am That I Am. Aum!

I Am one self united with my Creator. I Am That I Am. Aum!

I Am the light of the world. I Am That I Am. Aum!

I Am now a fully ascended being who has chosen to remain on
Earth to be of service to all sentient beings. I Am That I Am.
Aum!

Kodoish, Kodoish, Kodoish, Adonai 'Tsebayoth: Holy, Holy,
Holy is the Lord God of Hosts. Kodoish, Kodoish, Kodoish, Ado-
nai 'Tsebayoth: Holy, Holy, Holy, is the Lord God of Hosts. Ko-
doish, Kodoish, Kodoish, Adonai 'Tsebayoth: Holy, Holy, Holy,
is the Lord God of Hosts. I Am That I Am. Aum!

7 Divine Mother and Lady Masters Meditation and Activation

Close your eyes. Let us begin by taking a deep breath. Exhale.

We call forth the divine Mother and all the lady masters of the
Planetary and Cosmic Hierarchy. I now call to the divine
Mother and lady masters to supply a group merkabah in the
shape of a gigantic lotus blossom, which will carry us like a gi-
ant ocean liner sailing through the heavens and through the 352
levels of reality to the throne of the divine Mother.

Know that the divine Mother is the cosmic feminine being who is the left
hand of God and the fount from which all feminine goddesses and deities
spring forth. She is also the fount from which the feminine aspect of all beings
springs forth, including all of the gods, goddesses, ascended masters, initi-
ates, disciples—in actuality, every manifested aspect of creation.

Feel yourself being lifted up in the divine Mother's merkabah embrace
and carried upward through all the dimensions of reality to the very throne
of creation itself. As our lotus-blossom merkabah ascends to the 352d level of
divinity at the very heart of creation, we first experience absolute stillness and
all-pervading love. We are enveloped in a translucent platinum/pink light
that is now absorbing itself into every cell, molecule, atom and electron of our
being and into our soul and monadic essence.

We are also immersed in the most sublime fragrance of the sweetest
smelling roses we can imagine. In the background can be heard the music of
the spheres in the form of a radiant choir of angels singing ineffable, mag-
nificent melodies and harmonies. The light emanating from the throne of the
divine Mother is so bright that it takes a few moments for the eyes and senses

to adjust to such splendor.

As our eyes focus on the throne of the divine Mother, her translucent lighted form can now be seen, arms open to gather all into the center of her heart. It is as if the group has entered and become one with the living, pulsating heart of the divine Mother. As we remain in this stillness, we can feel our entire beings and hearts rhythmically beating to her cosmic pulse.

Know that the divine Mother and divine Father are but two halves of the same whole that together comprise that which we call the Godhead. Feel the exquisite love, joy, warmth, tenderness and nurturing within the divine Mother.

Feel yourself transforming into both an anchor for, and a transmitter of, this divine and hallowed love.

Know the safety and the nurturing that exists within this most sacred gift as the divine Mother continues to infuse you with the reawakening of this part of yourself that is the core of the Goddess within both female and male alike.

Now see within this translucent, hallowed, platinum/pink aura the blessed Virgin Mary as she glides to you upon a golden crescent moon. Feel the absolute purity of her essence and the wondrous benediction of her all-embracing love as she merges into this heart space in which you now find yourself.

She holds within her hand a pink rose representing love's tenderness, and individually hands one to each of you at this moment. She watches as you place the rose within your heart, thereby claiming the essence of the feminine spirit and of unconditional love for yourself.

Take a moment to feel this love flood through your being and then outward to touch all life.

Now see **Quan Yin** as she emerges out of the light. Feel her gaze penetrate you at every level of your being and flood you with the essence of divine mercy and compassion.

Take a moment now to let the purest qualities of compassion, mercy and forgiveness wash away any judgments or negativity that you have had toward self. Then let it spread outward to others in your personal life who are suffering due to lack of mercy, forgiveness and compassion. Let this same quality of compassion and mercy now flow outward to the entire planet as you join with Quan Yin in her holy service, spreading divine compassion, mercy and forgiveness.

See now **Pallas Athena** emerging from the light. Feel her quality of divine love and strength enter your being, recharging and reactivating these two aspects of the divine feminine as they commingle within her loving yet powerful essence. Take this in and know that her loving, tender, gentle, compassionate and nurturing feminine spirit also holds power, strength and command within it.

The feminine contains its unique brand of power and strength, yet these divine qualities are part of that which is the all-embracing divine Mother. Pallas Athena brings you the harmony of these energies in female form. Allow yourself to honor the divine feminine this moment by honoring Pallas Athena as well as your own feminine power, strength and command.

Watch now as a golden glow lights up your inner vision to unveil the face of Vesta, the feminine aspect of the Solar Logos. Let this golden glow stimulate the pure gold of your own true being as it pours forth and radiates out of Vesta. Allow yourself to connect with solar intent in a way that you have never before done on a conscious level. Feel the joy of knowing just how much a part of Vesta and this solar system of love/wisdom you truly are. Let this feeling now radiate outward into the cosmos.

Now see **Lakshmi** emerge upon her lotus blossom as she awakens within you the full knowingness that the abundance of all things is there for each one of you. She asks you now to think upon abundance and prosperity. Then hear her as she transmits to you the power to manifest your personal prosperity and abundance through the law of attraction. She wants you to know that you each have the power to do this by simply holding to the positive ideal of that which you seek, letting nothing sway you from this focused intent.

Allow yourself a moment to do this.

Now think of a situation or place within the sphere of the planet that is in need of prosperity and abundance and hold your positive, focused attention there for a moment.

See now the divine **Mother of the Native Americans**, who represents the soil, the grasslands, the rivers, oceans, mountains, trees, plants, animals and rocks. Allow all nurturing of Earth to flow through her into yourselves. Feel yourself anchor and activate her divine grace into the very core and heart center of our blessed planet.

Feel now the pervading presence of **Isis**. She breathes into each of you the breath of antiquity so that you may awaken to the new and ancient glory of your own Goddess energies. She emits from her aura the ability to decode the language of light, wherein the mysteries of your past, present and future stand forth to be revealed.

Now behold **Hera**, Greek goddess of wisdom. She waves her wand upon you that you may have the wisdom to use the ever-awakening truths and mysteries for the benefit of all humanity.

See now each of the **seven feminine archangels** as they one by one come to bless you with the distinct quality of their ray. First comes Faith, then Christine, Charity, Hope, Mother Mary, Aurora and Amethyst.

Pause and receive their specialized blessings.

*Now emerging are the **feminine elohim**: Amazonia, Lumina, Amora, Astrea, Virginia, Aloha and Victoria. Feel the enormity of their divine grace and blessing. Allow these most powerful cocreators within your field, and again drink deeply of the feminine strength and will to create.*

*See and feel the Goddess of Liberty, the Lady of Light, the Lady Nada, Parvati, Kali, Durga, Mary Magdalene, Portia, Mother Teresa, the Earth Mother, the Lady of the Lake, Lady Helena (formerly known as Madam Blavatsky) and the presence of **all the lady masters** who have ever graced and touched this planet.*

*See the **Gopis of Krishna** dance before you. Allow yourself to become one of them and dance with them as you embrace the feminine aspect of self. At this moment it does not matter if you are in male or female embodiment, for that which is of the Goddess lives within all of you and seeks to dance the great dance of divine love to the melodies of the flute of Krishna.*

Once again be aware of the breath flowing in and out of your heart center. Be aware also that there is a heart center located in a hidden chamber within the crown chakra. This is known as the "heart space within the head" and is one of the major access points where love and wisdom blend. The other major access point for the blending of these two energies is in the eye that is hidden in a secret chamber in the heart center. This point is known as the "mind within the heart."

Allow the breath now to flow evenly through your bodies while at the same time hold a point of focus in the heart within the head and the mind within the heart.

Simultaneously feel the solar plexus embrace the power of the feminine spirit. Know that this power is different from that which is contained with the masculine part of self and is also different from the power or will that is representative of the divine Father, divine masculine or yang energies. Each aspect, both feminine and masculine, has a point of balance within the other. So divine Mother and divine Father are complete within their own point of balance and yet are more fully complete when they merge their balanced essences within each other. The place where these two energies fully merge we call the Godhead.

Now take a moment to give thanks to the divine Mother. Give thanks also to the essence of the Goddess energy as she manifests within yourself, upon the Earth and all planes of existence. Likewise give thanks to the many lady masters, lady archangels and lady elohim who have given their blessings. Take a moment to give thanks to beloved Gaia, the Earth Mother. Now give thanks to the feminine spirit within each of your beloved brothers and sisters.

Finally, give thanks to the feminine spirit within yourselves, whether you are man or woman.

All the lady masters of the Planetary and Cosmic Hierarchy step forward and bring forth a love and light shower to all who reside in the lotus-blossom merkabah in the heart of the divine Mother. Feel and experience now the profundity of the cosmic feminine as her infinite forms rain down their blessings upon you. Completely soak in this love and light.

[One minute of silence.]

Now, beloveds of God, let us join our energies into this love and light shower and rain our collective love and light upon all our beloved brothers and sisters on Earth as well as on the Earth herself.

[One minute of silence.]

Bringing this process to a close, the divine Mother and lady masters gently and lovingly lift our merkabah out of the heart of the divine Mother and gently and caressingly glide us down the 352 levels of divinity back to Earth and into our physical bodies. As we return, feel the Earth Mother embrace us in gratitude and joy.

The divine Mother wishes you all to know that a part of you still remains in her heart, and she lovingly invites all to return in total consciousness anytime you feel the need or desire. She welcomes all her prodigal daughters and sons home in support of their service missions on Earth. She wants you to know that anywhere you are, there she is also. There is noplace in heaven or Earth where you are out of the divine Mother's embrace. Feel this, experience this, know this in the core of your being.

World Service Meditations

1 Planetary Axiatonal Alignment

As with all the following meditations, assume a comfortable position either sitting up or lying down with your spine straight. Sitting up is preferable because you are generally more focused. Leaning against a wall (if you are sitting on the floor) or the back of a chair is fine as long as the spine is straight. Lying down is also acceptable as long as you maintain your focus.

First request a personal axiatonal alignment so that you are as balanced as possible. Then request a full axiatonal alignment for Mother Earth. Visualize all the bodies of Earth totally and completely aligned, with all energies of our planet fully aligned with solar, galactic, universal, multiuniversal and cosmic divine intent. Relax and breathe slowly while holding the focus of a totally aligned, balanced and integrated Earth. Stay with this for up to five minutes as long as you feel comfortable.

2 Platinum Net Sweep

Begin by asking for the Platinum Net to sweep first over you and your group so that you are cleared of misqualified energies. Then request that the same be done for the planet as a whole. Request this for the physical, etheric, astral and mental atmosphere of the Earth so that each of her four lower bodies will receive one of the most potent cleansing, purifying and healing tools currently offered by the cosmic masters. Remain in meditation just long enough to fully visualize a gigantic platinum net sweeping over the four bodies of the planet and cleansing these bodies of debris. The more often this is done, the healthier the planet will become.

3 Meditation for the Earth Mother

When seated comfortably in your meditation position, call first for the overlighting presence of your own monad, then from that place, invoke all masters who work with the physical, etheric, astral and mental bodies of Earth. Call specifically on Lord Buddha, our Planetary Logos. Allow these wonderful healing energies to pour through you and fill your entire being. When you feel fully infused with these divine energies, anchor and activate your own grounding cord deep into the Earth. Turn your palms upward on your lap, or even extend your arms upward if you like. Ask that the healing currents of all the blessed masters whose presence you have invoked flow through you and outward into the Earth.

First visualize and direct these energies into the core of Mother Earth. Ask for a balancing and harmonizing in the foundation of the planet. Pour forth love so that all that needs healing will be healed, balanced and cleansed through grace rather than karma. Then put your attention on the Earth's etheric body. Ask all the masters present to help radiate through you their healing energies. Do the same for the astral atmosphere and astral body of the Earth so that all negative emotions are brought to a peaceful, loving calm. Then put your attention on the mental atmosphere or mental body of Earth. Send out only positive thought forms. Ask the masters to again bless and heal through you, and to infuse the mental world with their divine vision of positivity. Ask them to fill the mental atmosphere with their own outpicturing of the wondrous expression of the next millennium.

Let all these blessings come to harmony within yourself. Continue to meditate as long it feels comfortable, knowing that you are acting as a focal point for healing Mother Earth.

4 Political Hot Spots

There are definite political hot spots around the planet. The Middle East is certainly a key one, and has been for a long time. Bosnia is another. Russia is undergoing enormous stress, change and transformation. In fact, these political hot spots are so pervasive that I leave it to your discretion and personal attunement to select the ones you personally key into. Once you have done this, invoke the masters you are most connected with and the masters Saint Germain and El Morya.

Ask to be fully surrounded and protected by your semipermeable bubble of golden white light as well as the pure white light of the Christ. Then connect your third eye with your heart chakra. Next, align all your chakras, at the same time focusing on the third eye and heart. Hold in your mind's eye and your heart the political hot spot you have chosen. See all stresses and tensions melting away. Pray to the beloved masters, archangels, angels and elohim to help cocreate a peaceful and harmonious situation. Prayer is powerful in this world-service meditation; we are dealing with very delicate issues and want to be sure to invite the help of the masters. Call also on the angel of the country or countries you are focusing on. It is not necessary to know the name of the angel; just ask that the angel of that country or geographical area offer its assistance. Ask also for the assistance of the Arcturians and the Ashtar Command, and they too will assist within the limits of the law of non-interference.

Hold to your positive meditation for as long as you like. When you conclude, remember to thank the masters for their help, and remember to hold your positive imagery as you go about your day.

5 Social Issues

Each meditation done in world service should first be applied to self. Before beginning your meditation for social issues, for example, ask that any disharmony within your personal social life be brought into harmony. A simple prayer such as this helps integrate you in the service work you are doing for the world. It takes only a moment to make the request. Each of us is part of the world for which we are praying, so it makes perfect sense to ask for the same help in correcting personal imbalances that we are asking for the planet. Doing this will activate our own integration with the world. Please remember to include this basic format in each of your world-service meditations.

Once this is done and you are comfortably in your meditation position, pick a social issue to which you feel closely attuned. Examples might be the integration of the races, children in need of greater protection, starving children, all starving people, elevating the consciousness of society's youths, the elimination of gang violence and the pervasive issue of homelessness. There are, of course, others you might choose to focus on, as there is no shortage. Call on the masters of your choosing. The cosmic Avatar of Synthesis, the Mahatma, is an excellent being to call on, because one of his prime functions is to integrate his high-frequency energies into every level of existence. His power and presence is enormous, yet filters down to the most basic level of life. Call him in, beloved readers, for he can serve through each of you who does so.

Fix your attention on the social issue you have selected as your world-service meditation and begin to channel the love, light and will-to-good of God directly into the heart of that issue. See it transform within your inner vision from a situation of unfairness, disharmony and discrimination into a love-infused, light-infused expression of God. Feel the healing masters who work with these ideas pour their radiance through you. Feel the transformative and transmuting power of Saint Germain as he graces the situation with the light and fire of his violet transmuting flame. Feel the power of El Morya and Archangel Michael. Feel the immensity and enormity of the Mahatma energy, who, through your willingness to serve, easily transmits its energy to the situation at hand, uplifting and transforming that all may come into the highest possible expression of God at any given time.

Stay within the healing and peace of your service meditation until you feel complete. When you have concluded the meditation, always give thanks to the celestial Hierarchy who have helped you. Give thanks to your own soul and monad as well as to yourself for entering into such a meditation. Remember to continue to hold a positive focus on the issue you have prayed and meditated on. If the news confronts you with negativity or if you come face to face personally with the negativity you are seeking to transmute and heal, take note and then immediately shift gears to one of positive visualization and prayer. You are a healer here, and as any good physician does, you note the dis-ease, but devote all your energies on the cure.

6 Child and Spousal Abuse

Begin this meditation as you have been previously instructed. Ask for the proper protection and then ask that all abusiveness to self be transmuted. Surround yourself with a field of unconditional self-love. Then invoke your masters, including beloved Mother Mary, Quan Yin and Lord Maitreya.

This particular social issue has been singled out because it is a personal issue for many who suffer in silence. It is often well-hidden from all except those who are directly involved. By the power of this healing meditation, the required light and love will reach into those dark and hidden places. If there is a specific situation of this kind you wish to focus on, then do so. Otherwise, ask that your meditation go outward to anyone and everyone in need. This includes the abuser as well as the abused. Ask for the unconditional love of Mother Mary, the healing compassion and mercy of Quan Yin and the love/wisdom of the Christ to infuse all abusive situations. Also request the violet flame of Saint Germain that all misqualified energies contributing to the situation be transmuted.

Visualize now this unconditional love, wisdom. mercy, compassion and divine alchemy transforming these energies of abuse into energies of love. See and feel that which you have invoked entering into the surrounding field and hearts of all involved in this type of situation, quieting all storms and allowing wisdom and love to rule rather than uncontrolled anger. Focus this mostly on the perpetrator, not forgetting to ask for the compassion and mercy of Quan Yin to enter the hearts and minds of perpetrators who have been themselves abused. In order for a total healing to take place, all must ultimately be forgiven and brought to some form of harmony and peace. With the masters' help, we are trying to help heal the entire situation as completely as possible. This is a very sensitive area we have ventured into, and we do our best work through prayer and by requesting the divine intervention of the masters as long as the higher selves of those involved agree. The most appropriate way to do this work is to allow the masters to work through us.

These prayers are much needed, my beloved readers, and anyone who gives service time by requesting to be conduits for this healing energy will surely be blessed. At the conclusion of this meditation, be sure to ask to be cleared of any unwanted emotional energies you might have picked up.

7 Invocation to the Healing Angels

The healing angels are always ready to be of service to anyone who is ill or in the hospital or to come to the aid of anyone involved in an accident, natural disaster or any kind of harm. In truth, their divine presence can be seen and felt by those with inner vision in hospitals everywhere and around the ill and wounded. However, their work and their numbers would increase exponentially by our simple prayers and invocations.

Request their presence in your own life to help you with your own healing process. Then focus your attention either on a particular individual who is ill, a specific hospital, hospitals in general, or on any specific or generalized situation where their help is needed. Call on Archangel Raphael and Mother Mary to oversee this work. Then call the angels of healing in general and direct them to the area you have chosen.

For the benefit of those who are leading meditations such as these, the following is an example.

Close your eyes and assume a comfortable meditative posture, either sitting up or lying down. We now invoke the pure white light of the Christ and the semipermeable bubble of golden white light for protection. Only that which is good and of God can pass through this bubble. Only that which is of God can pass outward to our fellow human beings and to the planet. We are protected and act as conduits and servers for only the highest purposes.

We now invoke the blessed presence of Archangel Raphael and Mother Mary, his divine counterpart, to overlight this meditation.

We now invoke the presence of all of the angels of the healing arts.

We ask that every aspect of disharmony or dis-ease within our own bodies be bathed and washed clean within your healing light.

We now direct our attention to all hospitals around the globe.

We ask for the overlighting presence of Archangel Raphael and Mother Mary to infuse these hospitals so that all may be bathed within your blessed healing love-light.

We now ask for as many healing angels as needed to bring healing to all levels of the four lower bodies and to come and stand by the bedside of all who are suffering in hospitals everywhere.

We ask that you come in answer to our prayers and invocations, as long as the higher self of the individuals agree.

Please, oh blessed angels, pour forth all your divine healing force into everyone in need of you this moment.

Now let us be silent and allow the angels to work.
[Allow a few moments of silence.]

Now let us add our own love and healing energies to these places and the people in need while we ourselves are being healed by the force of the healing energies flowing through us.

[Allow another few minutes of meditation.]

We give thanks to you, Raphael and Mother Mary.

We give thanks to all the angels of the healing arts who are answering our heartfelt prayers at this moment. We ask that you stay as long as you are needed and that you continue to overlight any and all who are suffering. Amen, Amen, Amen.

When you feel ready, focus back into your bodies and open your eyes. Carry this peace and healing radiance within you as you leave this meditation, resume your own work and go about your day.

8 Invocation for Transitioning Souls

Close your eyes and find your meditative position.

We now call for a semipermeable golden white bubble of protection and for the pure white light of the Christ.

We ask that the little transitions that each of us here is going through serve to direct us to the highest light.

We call upon our higher self, monad, the inner-plane hierarchy of planetary and cosmic ascended masters, all archangels, elohim and God.

We ask that anyone [or insert a specific person's name] who is now going through their transition called death seek only the highest light.

We pray to their particular masters and guardian angels to help direct them to this light.

We pray also that they move quickly, gently and easily through their bardo experiences.

We ask that they know themselves to be the light and love of God and that they joyfully merge with the highest possible light of God radiance that presents itself to them.

We pray for their peace, joy, love and glory as they merge with the light of God and know themselves to be a flame of the ever-burning fire of God.

May their lives on the inner plane be filled with the love and light that embraces them and calls them home.

Kodoish, Kodoish, Kodoish, Adonai 'Tsebayoth!

9 Invocation to Liberate Earthbound Souls and Those Trapped in the Astral

Because the beginning of all meditations is the same, I am writing only the basics at this point. For greater detail, please study the above.

Close your eyes and assume your meditation position.

We now call for a semipermeable bubble of golden white light for protection.

We invoke the hierarchy of inner-plane planetary and cosmic ascended masters, the archangels and elohim.

In whatever way we each are personally bound to the Earth or trapped within the lower caverns of our astral nature, we now ask for the divine assistance of the masters to help to set us free.

On behalf of any of our brothers and sisters [specific trapped souls you may have encountered or know of can be named here] who are trapped within the lower astral realms and are tied or held to the Earth in any unhealthy manner, let them immediately be assisted to make their full transition to the inner planes to continue their evolution.

We ask and invoke the masters' and angels' aid to help awaken these earthbound souls to their situation so that they may willingly and joyfully let go of all attachments that no longer serve, and seek the their rightful place within the Father's mansions.

We pray that they accept the help being offered at this moment and joyfully find their higher purpose within the light. Amen.

We ask that any negativity or emotionalism we may have unknowingly taken in be immediately removed by the masters.

We give thanks and say Amen.

Sound three Oms.
Come back into the room and into the body. Open your eyes.

10 Invocation for Harmony between the Earth Kingdoms

Close your eyes and assume a comfortable meditative position.

We call forth our semipermeable bubble of golden white light for protection and ask to be surrounded by the pure white light of the Christ.

The light of Lord Buddha, his holiness Sai Baba, Krishna, Babaji and so forth can also be used. This depends on your connections and the tone of your group. Invoking the pure white light of the Christ has been used for a long time and is quite effective, so I am choosing to write the meditations in this format. Feel free to invoke any of the masters you wish.

We invoke the entire hierarchy of inner-plane planetary and cosmic ascended masters, all the archangels and elohim.

We set our intention to work in harmony with the nature spirits, devas, elementals and all of the angels and lesser builders as well as the archangels and elohim.

In your inner vision and imagination see the elementals and nature spirits at work within the grasslands, meadows, gardens, forests, oceans, lakes, rivers, within the currents and streams of air, wind and the movement of the seasons. See these beings dancing within the flames that heat our food and warm our bodies, and within the great fire of the Sun.

Breathe in unconditional love from your own mighty I Am Presence.

Now breathe this love outward to the other streams of evolution who share the work and glory of establishing the seventh golden age upon our world. Ask them to know us as beings of light and love, and acknowledge them as such beings.

We call upon the masters to help guide us that we may walk gently on the soil and ask that our actions be in harmony with the purpose of the whole, which includes the divine purpose of the nature spirits and elementals.

We ask to be guided and shown how to properly respect and honor them, and request the same from them that we may work in ever closer cooperation.

We especially invoke the guidance and direction of the great archangels and elohim.

Now meditate upon the love, joy and peace of this divine cooperation and integration.

[Allow some time for silent meditation.]

Come back into your body, infusing each cell with the joy, love, peace and harmony that we have meditated on.

Give thanks for the work of the nature spirits and elementals and for the lesser builders, the angels, the grace of the archangels and the elohim.

Establish your grounding cord within the Earth and in so doing make a deeper connection from spirit to Earth.

Now open your eyes.

11 Removing the Core Fear from the Earth and Humanity

Close your eyes and assume your meditation position.

We invoke our bubble of protection.

We call forth the hierarchy of inner-plane ascended planetary and cosmic masters, all archangels and elohim.

We call forth the presence of divine Mother and the lady masters.

We call forth Lord Buddha, Sanat Kumara and Vywamus.

We ask that the fear-matrix-removal program be activated for the collective body of humanity, including ourselves, and for the Earth Mother.

We request that any and all fear within the four lower bodies of Earth Mother and the collective body of humanity be completely removed.

Watch with your inner eye as these black weeds are taken from the field of the Earth Mother and lifted into the center of the violet fire of transmutation. All that is of a fearful and negative nature within the bodies of the Earth Mother and the collective of humanity are being transmuted into energy that shall be used only for positive purposes.

In place of the fear that has been removed, we now ask the divine Mother and lady masters to fill those spaces with unconditional divine love.

As part of the Earth Mother and the collective of humanity, feel this love filling your physical, etheric, emotional/astral and mental bodies.

We give thanks to the glorious beings who have assisted us in this work. Amen, Amen, Amen.

Extend a grounding cord deep within the Earth's core.
Send or channel love through that cord and feel the nectar of this divine love bathe you in its sanctified light.
Come back fully into the body and open your eyes.

12 Connecting the Consciousness of Humanity with the Extraterrestrials to Prepare for Open Dialogue

Close your eyes and assume your meditation position.
Invoke the bubble of protection, the pure white light of the Christ.

We call forth the hierarchy of inner-plane cosmic and planetary ascended masters, the archangels and elohim.

Open yourself now to the Confederation of Planets that has come from other worlds to assist the Earth in its evolution.
Now visualize the most spiritually attuned political leaders being elected into office.

We ask the Hierarchy to intercede in whatever manner that they are able in order to place lightworkers in these key political positions. We specifically request the help of El Morya and Saint Germain.

We now ask for the mass mind of humanity to begin to open to ever-greater awareness and acceptance of these benevolent beings who have come to aid us in our evolution.

Visualize all the lightworkers of the world becoming clearer in their attunements to the work of our extraterrestrial brothers and sisters.
Now see with your inner vision the governments of the planet openly communicating with our space brethren for the purpose of the betterment of Earth and the cooperation of our planet with divine intent.
Visualize clearly that the masses of humanity are now aware and educated regarding the reality and purpose of our space brothers and sisters, through the intervention of governmental leaders taking a stand for truth.
See with your inner vision how the lightworkers of the planet are able to work openly and collectively on their particular mission in mutual cooperation with the Confederation of Planets.
Feel the joy of all of humanity as well as that of our space brethren as we participate together in manifesting the plan of God and bringing the Earth forward into ever higher frequencies of light, love, power and the will-to-good.
Take a few moments now to connect with any incoming transmissions from this aspect of the celestial command. Even if we are not consciously hearing their intent, we are nevertheless receiving it through the universal language of light.

Bathe in this wonderful outpouring of grace and connectedness.
[Allow some time for silence.]

We now thank the celestial Hierarchy from other worlds who are here on humanity's behalf.

As we prepare to leave this meditation, hold the vision of lightworkers entering politics and being elected into the foreground both in the United States and in all the countries of the world.

Feel the joy of transformation through the mutual cooperation of humanity and the civilization and beings who form the Confederation of Planets.

Establish your grounding cord, come back into your body and open your eyes.

13 Invoking a Golden Cylinder

Close your eyes and assume your meditation posture.

We invoke the golden white semipermeable bubble of light for protection and the pure white light of the Christ.

We call forth the hierarchy of inner-plane ascended planetary and cosmic masters as well as the archangels and the elohim.

We now call forth the golden cylinder of light to envelop us within its cleansing and purifying radiance so that it may lift from within our personal auric fields any negative debris, negative elementals and thought forms, emotional currents or misqualified energy of any kind and remove it from our four lower bodies.

Now visualize within your mind's eye this golden cylinder growing larger and larger, merging with all the golden cylinders that you have invoked.

The golden cylinder keeps growing in size until it encompasses the entire planet, enveloping within its radiant sphere the collective bodies of humanity as they exist on the physical, etheric, astral and mental levels.

Now watch with your inner eye as the golden cylinder begins to draw upward all misqualified energy lodged within the dense physical vehicle of Earth until it reaches unimaginable heights, where it disintegrates into fragments of dust. See this dust, bathed within the golden light transformed into light patterns of energy.

Know within your minds and hearts that this once-misqualified or negative energy has now been transformed into pure light. Watch as it gently falls back to Earth as pure light substance, which acts as a stimulant for healing. Rejoice as you feel and see how what was once toxic, misqualified energy has been changed by the golden cylinder into a generator of light and healing.

Now see this process repeat itself as all etheric debris rises upward within the golden cylinder of light to be transformed into sparkles of light.

Watch and feel the transformation as this new transmuted energy falls from the mysterious heights to which the golden cylinder has carried it, back into the planet's etheric body to heal and regenerate.

Now see and deeply feel the impact of the same process as it repeats itself upon the astral plane. Watch as all negative emotional elementals that have been created from humanity's uncontrolled feeling body rise upward in the golden light cylinder. Feel the joy of unconditional love as these negative elementals return in a transmuted form, falling gently and sweetly back into the astral body of the planet as pink, white and golden hearts, tinged with the violet of transmutation. Take one of these hearts and place it within your own. Feel the impact of this most pure love. Taste the sweetness of transmutation as you fully realize that it is within the cocreative power of you and the God force to transform all negative and misqualifed energies into pure love and light.

Watch as this process repeats one final time. The golden cylinder sweeps upward the mass of negative thought forms and lifts them beyond harm's way, out of Earth's atmosphere. These thought forms are then transmuted into minute particles of light and gently rain down on the Earth's mental body, cleansing, clearing, purifying and helping to uplift and stimulate the minds of all.

Now the golden cylinder itself lifts up, getting smaller and smaller as it fades from sight. Sit for a few moments and bathe in the rarefied air that now pervades the collective consciousness of Earth and all humanity.

Meditate on the joy, love and lightness that pervades you and fills you.

[Allow a few minutes of silence.]

Ground yourself now fully into the physical body, extending your grounding cord within the Earth.

When you are ready, open your eyes, feeling refreshed and renewed.

14 Preserving the Rainforests and All Other Forests

Close your eyes and assume your meditation posture.

We invoke the golden white semipermeable bubble of protection and the pure white light of the Christ.

We call forth the inner-plane hierarchy of ascended planetary and cosmic masters, the archangels and the elohim.

Silently and within yourself bless the rainforests and ask that the masters and overlighting devas of the rainforests carry your personal prayer into the collective consciousness of those who have power to make decisions on the fate of the rainforests and all other forests.

*Now join with each other to form a group prayer that links you with those
who share the same concern over the preservation of the forests.*

**We call upon the Earth Mother to support us in this prayer. We
call once again on the overlighting deva of the rainforests and
all other forests to assist us in building a group thought form
strong enough to affect the thought forms of those who act to de-
stroy these sacred lands.**

**We ask that truth be revealed and that all may see and intuit
the preciousness of this hallowed ground, knowing that it is in
divine order that the rainforests be left to thrive.**

*Visualize these forests thriving healthily and functioning in wonderful
harmony with humanity and all the various kingdoms of evolution on this
planet.*

*Feel the blessings of Lady Gaia and that of the overlighting deva as they
support this visualization and do all within their power to help you manifest
your divine intention.*

*Allow yourself to smell the forest and feel the gentle breezes as they caress
you in love.*

Meditate for a few moments on the harmony of all nature.

[Allow time for silence.]

*Give thanks to all the various beings who help maintain the growth of all
forests and to the forests themselves.*

*When you feel ready, anchor and activate your grounding cord fully into
the Earth and send love and blessing through that cord into the core structure of the Earth.*

When you feel ready, open your eyes.

15 Protecting Endangered Species and Treating Animals with Love

Close your eyes and assume your meditation posture.

**We invoke the golden white semipermeable bubble of light and
the pure white light of the Christ for personal protection.**

**We call forth the inner-plane hierarchy of ascended planetary
and cosmic masters, all of the angels and the elohim.**

*Send a personal message of love and tenderness to yourself. Ask to be
cleared of all blockages that are a potential danger for you to freely and lovingly express who you are within the divine plan of God.*

**We now call upon beloved Master Kuthumi, who was in a past
incarnation Saint Francis. We call on gentle Jesus/Sananda,
who holds within his beingness the quality of pure devotion. We
call also on Quan Yin, goddess of mercy and compassion.**

We ask these wonderful beings to assist us in our meditation to protect the endangered species of our world, to help put a stop to animal abuse of every kind, and in its place promote the tender handling of the animal kingdom.

Visualize the animals of the wild roving freely about, following their natural instincts without interference by humanity. See the forests and jungles free and clear of any traps that could potentially harm these animals. Watch as they run wild and free.

Allow your visualization to expand and include tenderness to all animals. See alternatives imprinted on the mind of humanity that will allow the cessation of animal experimentation, replaced by benign forms of study. Hear within you the joy of the animals, who know they are free to follow their destiny without harmful interference by man.

Now let your thoughts and feelings drift to divine harmony between humanity and our animal brothers and sisters. See the animals being loved and cared for, living, learning, loving and evolving along with its human family.

Go deep within to the place where love alone dwells and to that time where the lion shall indeed lie down with the lamb.

Feel the joy that exists between the kingdom of humanity and the kingdom of animals.

Meditate on this harmony.

[Allow time for silence.]

Place your hands over your hearts that you may carry this love with you. Anchor your grounding cord, and when you are ready, open your eyes.

16 Removing Implants and Negative Elementals

Close your eyes and assume your meditation posture.

We invoke the golden white bubble of light and the pure white light of the Christ for personal protection.

We call forth the inner-plane hierarchy of planetary and cosmic ascended masters, the archangels and the elohim.

We call upon Vywamus, Lenduce, Djwhal Khul and Saint Germain to assist us to neutralize and eliminate all negative implants within our four lower bodies.

We thank you, beloved masters, and ask that you remain in order to help remove and deactivate all negative implants within all of humanity around the entire globe, as well as from within the fields of our pets.

We call upon Archangels Michael and Faith for extra protection.

We call upon the Lord of Arcturus and his fellow Arcturians for assistance, using their advanced technology.

We call also upon beloved Lord Buddha, our Planetary Logos, and on Sanat Kumara.

See, through your inner sense, pure golden light flowing into the mental, emotional, etheric and physical bodies of every person around the globe.

Watch as this light neutralizes every implant within the four lower bodies.

See this light become the hands of Vywamus, Sanat Kumara, Lenduce and Saint Germain as they lift these implants and elementals out of every aspect and area where they have been lodged.

That which is lifted by Vywamus, Lenduce and Sanat Kumara are transmuted by the touch of their golden light. The ones lifted out by the hands of Saint Germain are transmuted by his violet flame, which glows from within his hands. Djwhal Khul does this process through the use of his holographic computer.

Feel a lightness come over your entire being and let this lightness flow across the globe as you visualize all implants and negative elementals being either removed or made totally inactive.

We ask beloved Archangels Michael and Faith for extra protection against any further negative implants. We request this also from the Lord of Arcturus, giving permission for intervention.

We ask to be filled with the essence of pure love and radiant light and to be infused with the first ray of will. We request El Morya to assist us to strengthen our will power and that of all humanity, as the will of all merges with the will of God.

Know within the core of your being that pure unconditional love, pure light and the will-to-good act as barriers against any outside interference.

We invoke the added protection of archangels Michael and Faith now and each night before we sleep, for our further protection and the protection of all humanity and the animals companions who reside within our dwellings.

Return into your newly cleansed bodies. Remind yourself to stay centered within light, love and power, and build up an impenetrable force field of protection. Pray that all of humanity come to the understanding and application of divine law.

Thank all the beloved beings of the celestial realms who have assisted during this meditation.

Anchor your grounding cord and open your eyes.

17 Clearing All Interfering Astral Entities and Energies

Close your eyes and prepare for meditation.

Put on your semipermeable bubble of golden white light and invoke the pure white light of the Christ for protection.

We call upon the entire inner-plane hierarchy of ascended planetary and cosmic masters, all archangels and elohim.

We attune to our specific lineage of masters and to the master we work most closely with.

We ask these beings to help remove all unwanted astral entities, elementals or thought forms that cloud our vision, intuition, judgment, or who may be trying to interfere directly with our free will by clouding our perception.

We now ask the appropriate masters to help clear the unwanted astral entities, elementals or thought forms that are clouding the feeling and perception of humanity as a whole.

We ask that any astral entities engaged in direct interference with anyone's free thinking, clarity of vision or free will be immediately escorted to the astral sphere that best matches their vibratory rate. We ask that a ring-pass-not be placed around them to hold them there, so that they can learn their appropriate lessons and still be kept at a safe distance from meddling with humanity and our divine gift of free will.

See them being removed from both your personal sphere and the sphere of all of humanity while they are held in unconditional love. It is not our place to judge them, but it is certainly our right and even our obligation to ask them to be removed from our personal and collective worlds.

Feel a new clarity of feeling, thought, vision and intuition fill both you and the world of incarnated souls.

Sit and meditate on this feeling of freedom, clarity and light.

[Allow time for silence.]

Give thanks to your personal lineage of masters and the master or masters you have worked most closely with.

Thank all in the celestial Hierarchy who have aided in this process for everyone on Earth.

Anchor your grounding cord and open your eyes.

18 Healing the Four Bodies of Planet Earth

Close your eyes and assume your meditation posture.

Create your golden white bubble of protection and pure white light of Christ.

We call on the entire inner-plane hierarchy of ascended plane-
tary and cosmic masters, all archangels and all elohim.

We call on Helios and Vesta, Lord Buddha, Sanat Kumara, the
chohans of all the rays, the Manu, the Christ and the Mahacho-
han. We ask them for their healing radiance so that any auric
holes, leakages, spots and irritations within our four lower bod-
ies be healed.

We now call on the divine Mother, Lord Melchizedek, the Ma-
hatma and Archangel Metatron. We request that they and the
other masters radiate their cosmic healing energies to plug up
all leakages and auric holes, and clear up all spots and irrita-
tions in the physical, etheric, astral and mental bodies of the
planet.

Feel the divine aura surrounding and penetrating the entire planet as
you make this invocation. Feel health and vitality returning to the Earth and
all that dwell therein.

Sit and bathe in this divine radiance and benediction as you feel this
enormous healing and cleansing take place.

Drink in the aura of divinity within all your four lower bodies and all
your spiritual bodies as well.

Sit and meditate on the divine healing now occurring for the Earth and
for each of us who have prayed on her behalf.

[Allow time for silence.]

Anchor your grounding cord into the core of the Earth and radiate your
own love and light into her. Accept her all-encompassing love as she radiates
it to you through the stream of light moving through your grounding cord.

Silently and deeply thank all of the planetary and cosmic masters who
have aided the Earth in this healing.

Fully anchor back into your body and open your eyes.

19 Clearing All Planetary Illusion

Close your eyes and assume your meditation posture.

Put up your golden white bubble for personal protection and ask to be
clothed and protected in the pure white light of the Christ.

We call on the entire inner-plane hierarchy of planetary and
cosmic ascended masters, the archangels and elohim.

We first call on our own personal ascended-master lineage and
request that all personal glamour, illusion and maya be vac-
uumed up from the aura of our four lower bodies.

We now call forth the Mahatma, Melchizedek and Metatron and

*request their divine powers to vacuum up the mass conscious-
ness of glamour, maya and illusion that is affecting the planet
as a whole.*

*Watch as glamour, illusion and maya are lifted from the veil of delusion
of the entire planet.*

*See the Earth stand crystal clean and pure, radiating only that which is
true, holy, sanctified and of God.*

*As this process continues, bask in the glow of the radiance of these cosmic
masters.*

*Feel the incredible blessing of love, light and synthesis as the entire
planetary aura grows cleaner, clearer and ever more reflective of Source Itself.*

Meditate in silence and stillness upon the pure light and love of God.
[Allow time for silence.]

*Feel yourself become a greater and greater reflection of pure divine es-
sence while this is happening for the planet as a whole.*

*Give thanks to his holiness Lord Melchizedek, the Mahatma and Meta-
tron and to the group of ascended masters you have called on. Also give
thanks on behalf of each individual on planet Earth to all of the masters who
have participated in this clearing.*

*Anchor your grounding cord, feel yourself back in the body and open
your eyes.*

20 Clearing Atmospheric Pollution and Repairing the Ozone Layer

Close your eyes and assume your meditation posture.
Put up your golden white semipermeable bubble for protection.

**We call on the pure white light of the Christ and the entire
inner-plane hierarchy of ascended planetary and cosmic masters, all archangels and elohim.**

**We invoke the presence of Commander Ashtar and the entire
Ashtar Command as well as the Lord of Arcturus and the Arcturians who serve with him and ask that their advanced technology vacuum up all negative energies that form the personal
pollutants in our physical and etheric bodies, thereby increasing the purity of our bodies so that we can be a better vessel for
the service work we are now engaging in.**

*Allow a moment of silence as you visualize all negative energies within
your aura being vacuumed up by these wonderful beings. See these energies
lift from your four-body system on a stream of light that serves as a highly
developed etheric vacuum, to be taken from you and transmuted into harmless energy on their great ships. Trust their advanced technology to do this*

work and enjoy the feeling of lightness coming into your physical and etheric vehicles.

We now ask these combined energies to sweep across the entire planet, vacuuming up all physical pollution that has lodged itself within Earth's atmosphere on both physical and etheric levels.

Visualize their combined technologies creating a vacuum that spans the globe, and watch as all the pollutants that we have let loose within the physical/etheric atmosphere of our world are lifted up on this energy stream, to be rendered neutral and harmless aboard their ships.

Feel a wonderful sense of purity and cleanliness pervade the entire planet.

We ask that these advanced technologies help repair the ozone layer around the globe.

Know in your heart that by your making this request, they will give all the help they can. They cannot, however, act without being asked, so feel the joy of making these requests, for you are helping to create the world as God would have it.

Sit in meditation for a while, feeling a lightness, purity and healing take place within both your own physical vehicle and that of the physical/etheric body of the Earth.

Visualize all the pollutants being vacuumed out of Earth's atmosphere and feel the incredible love and compassion of the wonderful beings who have responded to our request.

Enjoy the feeling of increasing lightness, purity and love that fills you and radiates around the globe at this time.

[Allow a few moments for silence.]

Give thanks to the Lord of Arcturus and Commander Ashtar and all those who work beside them.

When you have done this, anchor and activate your grounding cord, feel yourself fully in the body and open your eyes, feeling cleansed and refreshed.

21 Anchoring Earth's Monadic Blueprint

Close your eyes and assume your meditation posture.

Put up your golden white semipermeable bubble of light and call upon the pure white light of the Christ.

We call on the entire inner-plane hierarchy of ascended planetary and cosmic masters, all archangels and all elohim.

We invoke the presence of beloved Melchior, Helios and Vesta, Sanat Kumara and Lord Buddha.

We now call upon the particular master or masters with whom

we each work for a full and complete anchoring of our personal monadic blueprint body.

Feel the activation, joy, love and light while this is being installed deep within you.

Meditate for a moment on this feeling. Feel also the tingling sensation as the language of light is activated within you and as all key codes, sacred geometries and fire letters are fully installed and stimulated.

We now ask that the monadic blueprint body be anchored into and around the entire globe.

We call for the help of beloved Saint Germain to help in this process and request that the divine monadic blueprint body be anchored within Earth for the full manifestation of the new millennium.

We ask that all who are ready now have access to the language of light and that the highest possible activation of all key codes, sacred geometries and fire letters be given to those on the planet who are able to receive them.

Sit now for a few minutes in silent meditation as you visualize this great downpouring of light, the anchoring of the planetary monadic blueprint body and the installation and activation of the key codes, fire letters and sacred geometries around the globe.

[Allow a few short moments of silence.]

Know that the divine celestial masters will bestow the highest that each may personally receive and that your prayers and invocations are helping to accelerate safely the evolution of the globe and to anchor in the new millennium.

Meditate and enjoy this feeling.

[Allow time for silence.]

Give thanks to all the masters who have helped in this sacred process.

Feel yourself aligning with your own monadic blueprint body and fully integrating within your twelve-body system.

Anchor yourself back into your mental, emotional, etheric and physical vehicles.

Anchor your grounding cord and open your eyes.

22 Invoking a Shower of Core Love and Core Light

Close your eyes and assume your meditation posture.

Put up your semipermeable bubble of golden white light for protection and call upon the great white light of the Christ.

We call on the entire inner-plane hierarchy of ascended planetary and cosmic masters, all archangels and all elohim.

We invoke the presence of the divine Mother and all the lady masters, focusing on their glorious heart energy.

We call and invoke now the divine Father and all the masculine energies, focusing on their attribute of light.

We call specifically on his holiness the Lord Sai Baba, Melchizedek, the Mahatma and Metatron.

Now connect yourself with all your brothers and sisters on the planet.

See and feel your interconnectedness with the Earth herself and with every kingdom evolving on her hallowed soil, within her waters, in the air and within her fires.

In this state of unity we call forth to all the celestial Hierarchy for a shower of Core Love and Core Light to come forth from the very heart/mind of the Godhead.

Feel the divine outpouring of the purest essence of love that you have ever felt. Take this love deep into your heart. Infuse every cell, atom and electron of your twelve-body system with it.

Feel the immensity and enormity of this Core Love as it pours forth into every being and aspect of creation upon the planet.

[Allow a few moments of silence.]

Now feel and see the essence of Core Light as it streams forth from the eternal fire of God. Feel this light infuse every cell, atom and electron within your twelve-body system.

Feel the immensity and enormity of this Core Light as it streams forth into every being and aspect of creation on the planet.

Sit for a few minutes in silence and bask in the radiance of Core Love and Core Light as it blesses and graces both you and the entire world.

[Allow 5 to 10 minutes of silence.]

With deepest reverence give thanks to the divine Mother and the divine Father and all of the celestial realms who have given of themselves in order to assist in this benediction.

Feel yourself coming fully into your mental, emotional, etheric and physical body.

Anchor your grounding cord within the love- and light-infused Earth and open your eyes.

6

Celebrating the Holy Days

My beloved readers, there are nine holy days that the inner-plane ascended masters have asked me to write special classes for. These
nine holidays, or holy days, are Wesak, the Festival of the Christ, the Festival of Humanity, Christmas, Easter, Thanksgiving, Jewish holidays, Sai Baba's birthday, ten additional full moons, the spring and fall solstices and the
fall and winter equinoxes. I will first share the format of the celebrations of
the ascended master high holy days followed by the structure for the specific classes.

Wesak

Your Wesak ceremony can begin with the opening I outlined in chapter
1. The only addition is the masters' suggestion that you use the prayer, the
Affirmation of the Disciple, at the end of the opening. Since Wesak (also
known as the Festival of the Buddha) is the high point of incoming spiritual
energies for the year, the masters have recommended two meditations instead of one, as most holidays and classes have. First, read the following introduction.

Introduction to the Wesak Festival

The Wesak Festival is the most important of the three major ascended-
master festivals. It is the time of the year at the Taurus full moon when humanity receives the highest frequency of light. Wesak is a living event
based on current astrological cycles, not past events that occurred centuries
ago, as most religions celebrate. The Wesak Festival is the Festival of the
Buddha, commemorating the anniversary of his birth, his attainment of
buddhahood and his ascension. The Buddha, the perfect expression of the
wisdom aspect of God, is the embodiment of light and divine purpose.

This is the great Eastern festival, and serves to show the solidarity of
East and West. The term "Wesak" refers to the Wesak Valley in the Himalayas, where every year all the ascended masters gather on both the inner
and outer planes to share in a sacred ceremony. At the precise rising of the

full moon in May, the Manu Allah Gobi; Lord Maitreya, the Christ; and Saint Germain, the Mahachohan, stand in a triangular formation around a bowl of water that sits on a crystal. Buddha appears, hovering above this bowl of water, transmitting cosmic energies into the water and through Lord Maitreya to be disseminated to the Spiritual Hierarchy and the initiates, disciples and new group of World Servers.

At the end of the ceremony the water is shared by all those in attendance. Wesak is also the time when initiations are given to the disciples on Earth by Lord Maitreya, Lord Buddha and more recently by Lord Melchizedek, the Universal Logos.

The Wesak is a time of great renewal and celebration. The quality of energy is the "force of enlightenment." This energy emanates from the heart of God and is related to divine understanding and the love/wisdom aspect of God. On a planetary level it initiates the new world education.

This affects educational movement, values, literature, publishing, television, radio, newspaper, magazines, writers, teachers and speakers on the entire planet. This force of enlightenment so prevalent at Wesak is why large groups coming together at this time can be such an awesome experience. Wesak is where the greatest window for mass enlightenment can occur on a planetary level.

During the ceremony Buddha sounds forth a great mantra and becomes an absorbing agent of the first-ray force. Buddha then uses the magnetic power of the second ray to attract this force to himself. He holds it steady and then redirects it to Lord Maitreya, who is the receiving agent of this energy. This energy is then disseminated to the seven chohans and their ashrams for a sevenfold expression and direction into the world.

All the disciples and initiates on Earth are invited to come to the Wesak Valley, attend this sacred ceremony and join in the festivities. This is also a time to come and stand before Lord Maitreya, Lord Buddha and Sanat Kumara to give your vows of service and receive special blessings.

The Wesak Festival has been regarded by the inner-plane ascended masters to be of paramount importance in world affairs. Through the two representatives of deity on our planet, the worlds of spiritual realities and human affairs are being brought closer and closer together.

Many people have dreamed of this event but have not known its spiritual significance and where or why they were doing what they were doing in the dream. At Wesak a channel is opened for humanity that allows disciples and initiates to contact certain energies not normally available or as easily accessible. This allows great expansions of consciousness to take place.

Djwhal Khul has also stated that "It is the intention of the Buddha and the Christ that in each country there shall eventually be someone who will act as their representative at the time of the two festivals, so that the distribution of spiritual energy from the first great aspect or ray will be directed from the Buddha to the Christ and then from the Christ to those initiates in every country who can be overshadowed, and so act as channels for the direct current of energy." This references the Festival of the Christ and the Wesak Festival.

Djwhal Khul, in the Alice Bailey book, *Ponder on This*, also has said about the Wesak: "No cost is too great to pay in order to be of use to the Spiritual Hierarchy at the time of the full moon of May, the Wesak Festival. No price is too high in order to gain the spiritual illumination which can be possible, particularly at that time."

The Wesak has four basic functions:

1. To substantiate Christ's continued physical appearance on Earth.

2. To physically prove the solidarity of the Eastern and Western approaches to God.

3. To form a rallying point and meeting place for those who annually, both literally and symbolically, link up and represent the Father's house, the kingdom of God and humanity.

4. To demonstrate the nature of the work of Christ as the great and chosen intermediary and leader of the Spiritual Hierarchy and the disciples and initiates on Earth. He voices the Hierarchy's demand for the recognition of the factual existence of the kingdom of God here and now (see Alice Bailey's *Ponder on This*, pp. 422-423).

The purposes of the Wesak Festival are as follows:

1. The releasing of certain transmissions of energy to humanity that will stimulate the spirit of love, brotherhood and goodwill.

2. The fusion of all men and women of goodwill into a responsive, integrated whole.

3. The invocation and response from certain cosmic beings if prior goals are achieved.

I would like to end this section with one final quote from Djwhal Khul on the Wesak from a passage in Alice Bailey's *The Rays and Initiations II*. "If you have faith as a grain of mustard seed in what I have told you, if you have a staunch belief in the work of the spirit of God and in the divinity of man, then forget yourselves and consecrate your every effort, from the time you receive this communication, to the task of cooperation in the organized effort to change the current of personal and world affairs by an increase in the spirit of love and goodwill in the world during the month of May."

Through the Buddha the wisdom of God is poured forth. Through the Christ, Maitreya, the love of God is made manifest to humanity. This festival links the work of the Buddha and the Lord Maitreya symbolically and literally.

(This is not the first time that Lord Maitreya and Lord Buddha have joined together. It should be remembered by those who have studied Eastern religion that Lord Maitreya was the great avatar Lord Krishna in a past life and Buddha was at that time his disciple, Arjuna. Their work together continues now in a much more cosmic and expanded form.)

This is a time of enormous blessings being poured forth to the disciples, initiates, new group of World Servers and humanity on Earth. As the masters, initiates and disciples leave the ceremony, they are filled with a sense of renewed strength to undertake another year of world service. Are you beginning to see, my friends, the enormous importance of the Wesak Festival?

From the perspective of the ascended masters, it is the single greatest event on our planet, one that has the greatest effect on the human race. It is also in this time that the lodge of masters meets on the inner plane for the following four reasons (outlined by Djwhal Khul in the Alice Bailey books): "To contact spiritual force, which is transmitted to our planet through the medium of the Buddha and the Christ; to confer together as to the immediate necessity and the work to be done for humanity; to admit to initiation those who are ready; and to stimulate their disciples to increased activity and service."

Can you imagine the effects on this planet when all humanity consciously celebrates the Wesak Festival? In recent times a call has been sent out by the entire Spiritual Hierarchy of ascended masters to all initiates and disciples and new group of World Servers to prepare themselves at each May full moon for an intensive holy month of accelerated service. This effort is to increase the receptivity of humanity to the new spiritual forces released at this time.

The actual Wesak focus has recently been extended to cover five days for work and service: the two days prior to the full moon, the day of the festival itself, and the two days after the Wesak ceremony. The two days of preparation are called the Days of Renunciation and Detachment. The day of the festival is called the Day of Safeguarding, and the two succeeding days are called the Days of Distribution. This demands five days of intensive service. (This is why the masters have guided us to hold our celebration for Wesak at Mount Shasta for three days, with an additional day before and after for traveling, which prepares and then integrates the collective group experience.)

Your Wesak Ceremony

After reading the preceding introduction, read the Meditation in the Golden Chamber of Melchizedek beginning on page 34. (I do not have this one on audio tape yet, so you can read it aloud or tape it in advance of the class.) This meditation takes about an hour and is extremely powerful. It may be the most powerful meditation I have ever channeled. It is tied to the "Updated God Ascension Seat Meditation."

Take a 15-minute break. Then begin the ceremony. Call forth to the Planetary and Cosmic Hierarchy for your class members to be connected with the Wesak ceremony going on in the Himalayas, as enacted by Lord Buddha, Lord Maitreya and the inner-plane ascended masters. Then also request to be connected to the major global event I host in Mount Shasta. Third, request that your class be connected to all Wesak celebrations worldwide. After asking the class to prepare for meditation, play the audio tape of an actual Wesak ceremony I have made for this purpose (about 30 minutes) or read the guided meditation that follows. After this meditation experience and the soul-travel to the Wesak Valley in the Himalayas, take fifteen or twenty minutes for the class members to share their experiences.

Last is the closing ceremony described in chapter one. Allow extra time for socializing afterward. Since it is a holiday, it might be appropriate to have a potluck before or after the class. There should be no charge for this class, since it is considered by the masters to be one of the holiest days of the year.

How to Structure Your Wesak Ceremony

The most important part of this celebration is reading the following ceremony (or playing the audio tape). If you have three hours, I recommend that the first hour be spent reading about Wesak, the second hour doing the Meditation in the Golden Chamber and the third hour doing the ceremony. Obviously you will have breaks between these three segments. If you have only two hours, skip the Golden Chamber meditation and just read the introduction to Wesak followed by a discussion. Then do the Wesak meditation that follows.

The Wesak Ceremony Meditation

Close your eyes. Take a deep breath. Exhale.

We again call forth the Planetary and Cosmic Hierarchy to help in this meditation.

We call forth the full opening of all our chakras, including the ascension chakra, which sits at the back of the head [*where a ponytail is fastened*].

The meditation experience we now begin is the highlight of the entire Wesak celebration. Let us now prepare ourselves for this holy and sanctified experience with a moment of silence.

We now call forward our inner-plane spiritual hosts and ask for a group merkabah, which is like a gigantic boat that will take

all present, both on the inner and outer planes, to the Wesak Valley.

Let us now soul-travel together to the actual Wesak Valley in the Himalayas to experience the Wesak ceremony conducted by the inner-plane ascended masters.

Feel yourself descending into the Wesak Valley, joining all the other ascended masters, initiates and disciples already gathered there.

See and/or feel the presence of Lord Maitreya, the Planetary Christ, and Saint Germain, the chohan of the seventh ray and new Mahachohan.

See these three masters standing in a triangle around a bowl of water that sits upon a very large crystal.

Also see Allah Gobi, known as the Manu, who holds the first-ray position in the Spiritual Hierarchy. See, feel and/or visualize all the rest of the masters of the Spiritual Hierarchy standing in a circle around these three masters.

As the full moon is still just below the horizon, the excitement builds as all await the arrival of Lord Buddha. As the moon now begins to rise, a stillness settles upon us, and we all look toward the northeast. Certain movements and mantras sound forth under the guidance of the seven chohans of the seven rays.

In the northeast a tiny speck can be seen in the sky. It gradually grows larger and larger and the Buddha becomes discernible, seated in a cross-legged position. He is clad in a saffron-colored robe and bathed in light and color, with his hands extended in blessing.

While Buddha hovers above the bowl of water, a great mantra is sounded by Lord Maitreya, one that is used only once a year at Wesak. This invocation sets up an enormous vibration of spiritual current, marking the supreme moment of intensive spiritual effort of the entire year for all initiates and masters present.

Let us watch as Lord Buddha hovers over the bowl of water, transmitting his divine cosmic energies into it and through Lord Maitreya. The energy is then sent forth by Lord Maitreya to the entire Spiritual Hierarchy and into all of us who form a part of this hierarchy on Earth.

Feel this massive downpouring of cosmic energies from the Planetary and Cosmic Hierarchy, flowing not only through us, but also flowing out into the world and into the Earth herself.

As these energies continue to pour in, see the bowl of water, taken from the crystal, being passed around the crowd. See and feel yourself sipping this holy, blessed water.

See yourself now walking toward Lord Buddha, Lord Maitreya and Sanat Kumara, our previous Planetary Logos, who now overlights Buddha in his new position in the spiritual government.

Stand now before these three loving masters and share with them on the inner plane what you feel your service work, mission and puzzle piece is in God's divine plan on Earth. Take this time to make any requests to God and these three masters for help for self or for others and in manifesting your mission.

Let us now take 30 seconds of silence to allow you to make these prayer requests.

Feel and visualize these prayers being answered, and thank Lord Buddha, Lord Maitreya and Sanat Kumara for their guidance and blessings.

Find yourself walking now in the Wesak Valley toward a less populated and very beautiful nature spot. Have a seat and allow yourself to just be, resonating with all that has taken place.

Take a moment now to feel the full joy and blessings of this moment and of the entire Wesak ceremony, and allow this feeling to become embedded into the core of your being. Know that all of us and the entire hierarchy of inner-plane ascended masters are one.

Find yourself now looking toward the ceremonial circle and gathering near the large crystal and bowl. See, feel and visualize Lord Buddha beginning to rise in the lotus posture, floating back to the northeast to the realm from which he came.

As Lord Buddha again becomes a small speck in the distance, see and feel the arrival of our inner-plane spiritual hosts with their gigantic group merkabah. Feel yourself now joining this merkabah in total oneness, joy and love.

Feel the group merkabah, floating through space and time, return you back to your physical body.

Before opening your eyes, take one last moment to send love to all our brothers and sisters present, who have shared this journey and this Wesak celebration with us. Let us send and receive this love now.

Let us now call forth from the inner plane his holiness the Lord Sai Baba, the cosmic Christ, to give his final blessing and benediction and close this Wesak ceremony by sprinkling his sacred vibhuti ash etherically upon all present. Let us receive this final Wesak ceremony blessing now.

When you feel complete, open your eyes.

Djwhal Khul on the Wesak Celebration

Beloveds, I come to you in Buddha's sacred name to once again call your attention to the celebration of Wesak, to the sacred and sanctified energies that are released to humanity and to this blessed planet on the night of the Taurus full moon. The details of this sacred ceremony have been unveiled to you through the writing of certain select teachers, as this hallowed festival of the Buddha was sought to be imprinted on humanity's conscious minds. It is not the details I hereby step forward to speak of, but the intent behind the more recent revelations concerning Wesak.

In the not-too-distant past, this most sacred of ceremonies has stayed behind the veil of conscious participation, remaining outside the awareness of humanity's conscious minds. Although attended on the inner planes by many of you, little if any recollection was brought to your awareness. Now, with the dawn of the new millennium practically visible on the horizon, it is time for Wesak to enter into your conscious world. The hour has struck, my dear friends, and slowly the veil is being lifted. It is already lifted well enough that each of you has the choice to consciously ask to participate in the moment of exchange between Lord Buddha, now wearing the mantle of Planetary Logos, and Lord Maitreya, the planetary Christ. You are conscious enough to humbly yet gloriously stand forth and with full intent sip from the sanctified waters. You are now beginning to avail yourselves of the wondrous spiritual benedictions and energies that flow out this holy evening, when all of the celestial Hierarchy bathe in the field of liquid light and in joyous yet sacred ceremony celebrate and replenish for another year filled with divine service and mission.

This new millennium has gathered around itself the force and momentum that shall see the manifestation of God upon the Earth. As more and more of you gather together in physical embodiment in larger and larger groupings, such as the group that gathers at Mount Shasta to honor and celebrate the Wesak, more and more of heaven is anchored on Earth. It is for this reason I come to you, to honor and enlighten you, oh blessed brothers and sisters in God. Know that by making the merest inquiry regarding this divine outpouring, you are taking one step closer toward anchoring the holy Wesak in the physical. By joining together in groups and actively participating with full conscious intent in this sacred hour, you have and are acting as the holy anchors of manifestation of the kingdom of God on Earth. I join with all my brothers and sisters in God to celebrate this Wesak celebration. I join with you as you in turn join with the inner-plane hierarchy of masters, who ourselves join with blessed Lord Buddha and beloved Lord Maitreya. Together our vibrations of love joyfully infuse Earth's very core, and the heights of that which you call the heavens with the glory of the Most High.

This is why I say I honor you. This is why the masters all honor you, as does the Christ, as does beloved Lord Buddha, as do the cosmic masters who join their forces with our own in the transformation of this planet into an orb of light. Thus as the seventh golden age enters its hour of dawning, we all stand together as one, drinking from the fount of divine light as one and moving the world forward as one. You are all beloveds of all the masters, and you are all blessed.

The more that the Wesak celebration is physically anchored upon the solid soil of Earth, the deeper the penetration of the sacred energies into the core of Earth herself. I take my leave, yet remain in gratitude to all who participate in the holiness of Wesak. — Djwhal Khul

The Festival of the Christ

The next major holiday the ascended masters would like you to celebrate is the Festival of the Christ, which occurs at the full moon in April, or the full moon one month prior to Wesak. (If there is any confusion, call my office and we will give you the exact dates.)

Begin this ceremony with the standard class opening as described in chapter 1. The ascended masters recommend repeating out loud The Great Invocation (pp. 3-5) three times, the Lord's Prayer (pp. 5-6) three times and either the Traditional Rosary once or the New Age Rosary twice. (pp. 6-8). When this process is complete, read together the following introduction to the Festival of the Christ, then do the guided meditation that follows.

Introduction to the Festival of the Christ

This is the festival of the living and risen Christ. This is not referring to the Master Jesus, but the Lord Maitreya, who overlighted Jesus and shared his body during the last three years of his life.

Lord Maitreya is the planetary Christ, head of the Spiritual Hierarchy, teacher to all the ascended masters and a galactic avatar. This festival celebrates the life of Jesus and the resurrection example that the Master Jesus and Lord Maitreya set and have built on the last 2000 years. Lord Maitreya is the perfect embodiment of the love expression of God.

The forces of restoration are particularly active at the time of the Festival of the Christ. These restorative forces emanate from the mind of God and are connected with the principle of active intelligence. This energy stimulates mass intelligence and the birth of form. It makes people think, plan and take action along spiritual lines. On a planetary level this energy will eventually lead to a reorganization of planetary life. The effects are primarily physical, with the object of creating heaven on Earth.

The keynote of the festival is **love**, in the highest sense of this term. The second keynote is **resurrection**. The third keynote is **contact**. This refers to a closer relationship with Lord Maitreya and his disciples and initiates and a closer relationship between the Spiritual Hierarchy and humanity. This festival lasts for three days and prepares the way for the Wesak Festival. At this time Lord Maitreya sounds the Great Invocation, first alone, then with the united Spiritual Hierarchy.

Meditation for the Festival of the Christ

Close your eyes and sit as comfortably as you can, holding the spine erect.

Center your attention at the heart chakra and begin to breathe easily and naturally through that center as if there were a nose in the middle of your chest.

Visualize the heart center opening like a beautiful flower, as you continue to breathe love in and out (it is pink).

See the image of the heart of Christ within your own heart. Continue to breathe.

Now focus your attention at the top of your head, with your gaze turned inward and upward toward the third eye. Visualize the pure white light of the Christ flowing into the crown chakra.

Now visualize the pure white light of the Christ merge with the beautiful pink light of love. Feel this luminous, gentle pink-white light begin to flow throughout your entire four-body system, then into your entire twelve-body system.

Feel yourself merge in totality with the energy and being of Christ himself. Feel the incredible love, devotion and illumination become your very self.

Inwardly kneel at the altar of your own christed self. Know that this is your own true nature.

Let your christed self bow to Lord Maitreya, beloved master Jesus/Sananda and Kuthumi. Know that in this moment they are bowing to your Christ self even as you are bowing to theirs.

Realize that the entire planet is an aspect of Christ waiting to wake up to the realization of its divinity, each human's oneness with the One.

Inwardly bow to the christed nature of the entire planet, and know that as you are doing this, you are likewise bowing to the buddhic nature of all things. Realize that in truth you are simply bowing to the divine nature of all that exists.

Feel the energies of divine love within you pouring outward to the entire planet. See this beautiful, softly luminous pink-white light touching and enveloping everything in the sublimest form of love. Know that you and all are forever held within the aura of this love.

Bring your attention back to the heart center. Follow your breath as it flows easily in and out of this center. Inwardly offer thanksgiving for the experience of the glorious love of the Christ. Inwardly offer this love as a blessing to the planet as a whole and to any situation of a planetary or personal nature that you feel is most in need of this beatific energy.

Know that you are able to access this glorious love anytime you want, as well as direct it to any situation, person or circumstance you feel directed or guided to. Know that you can do this because you are a perfect son/daughter of the Father/Mother God.

Keeping the essence of this love inside you, slowly become aware again of your surroundings. Allow the love to anchor you to your physical surroundings and the Earth.

When you feel ready, open your eyes.

Know that all that you see, beloved brothers and sisters, is but an aspect of the divine in form. Walk through the world knowing that all is forever blessed within the light and love of the Christ.

Take a 15-minute break.

After the break the masters have recommended that you play the audio tape called "Core Love Meditation" or alternatively, read the meditation, Invoking a Shower of Core Love and Core Light, beginning on page 75.

After completing this, take 15 to 20 minutes for personal sharing. Then go through the closing ceremony beginning on page 9. Since this is a high holy day, you might consider having a potluck or supplying some extra refreshments and snacks.

The Festival of Humanity

The Festival of Humanity occurs at the full moon after the Wesak Festival. (You can call my office to get the exact date.) This ceremony should start with the standard opening in chapter 1. The masters suggest that in this opening ceremony the expanded version of the Great Invocation should be used (p. 4). The ascended masters also suggest reading the prayer Affirmation of the Disciple (pp. 8-9) together out loud. (If I haven't said this already, all prayers should be said in unison.) The ascended masters also recommend reciting the Prayer of Saint Francis (pp. 5-6).

On completion of the opening ceremony, please read aloud the following short description of the Festival of Humanity.

Introduction to the Festival of Humanity

The Festival of the Spirit of Humanity aspires towards divinity, attunement to God's will and right human relationships. It occurs each year at the full moon in June. It is a day to recognize and honor the divine nature of humanity and aspire toward spiritual fellowship. This festival represents the effects in human consciousness of the work of Gutama Buddha, Lord Maitreya and the Master Jesus. This festival has also been recognized as World Invocation Day.

The force prevalent at this festival is the force of reconstruction. This is the force of the first ray, or will aspect of divinity that is directly connected with Shamballa. This force is mainly effective between nations of the Earth.

Its effect on a given nation is governed by that nation's level of evolution. The two extremes are ego-centered nations versus nations focused on world unity. The United Nations is one manifestation of this force in its more positive aspect. The three forces of *restoration, enlightenment,* and *reconstruction* express the light, love and knowledge of God. The synthesis of these forces and the effects of these festivals consciously celebrated by humanity will produce the following results, as outlined by Alice Bailey in her book, *Serving Humanity*:

1. Power will be given to the disciples and initiates so that they can direct efficiently and wisely the process of rebuilding.

2. The Will to Love will stimulate men of goodwill everywhere, gradually overcoming hatred. The inner urge in men and women to live together cooperatively already exists and is subject to stimulation.

3. The Will to Action will lead intelligent people throughout the world to inaugurate those activities which will lay the foundation for a new, better and happier world.

4. The Will to Cooperate will steadily increase. Men and women will desire and demand right human relationships as a natural way of life.

5. The Will to Know and to Think Correctly and Creatively will become an outstanding characteristic of the masses. Knowledge is the first step toward wisdom.

6. The Will to Persist will become a human characteristic, a sublimation of the basic instinct of self-preservation and self-centeredness. This will lead to a persistent belief in the ideals presented by the Spiritual Hierarchy and the demonstration of immortality.

7. The Will to Organize will further a building process which will be carried forward under the direct inspiration of the Spiritual Hierarchy. The medium will be the potency of the Will to Good of the new group of World Servers and the responsive goodwill of mankind.

When the process of reading this section is complete, the ascended masters recommend reading chapter 16 in *The Complete Ascension Manual (Vol. 1)*, "Sanat Kumara and the Planetary Hierarchy." This takes about 40 minutes. Then take a break.

After the break, play the audio tape meditation called "Ultimate Ascension Activation Meditation," or read the Ascension Meditation and Treatment beginning on page 45. Afterward, take fifteen minutes for sharing. Then do the closing ceremony in chapter 1. When the session is over, you could have a potluck or perhaps extra refreshments for the holiday.

A Christmas Ceremony

The masters have guided me to celebrate Christmas in the following manner. Begin with the standard opening, then add the Lord's Prayer (repeated three times) and the Rosary (repeated three times), either the traditional or the New Age version. The masters also recommend reciting the long version of the Great Invocation, then possibly reading some of your favorite Bible passages or passages from *A Course in Miracles*. Next, read chapter 14 in *The Complete Ascension Manual*, "The Untold Story of Jesus the Christ," all of which should take about an hour or less. When this is complete, take time for sharing. Encourage people to ask questions and have discussions during these readings, then take a 15-minute break.

After the break do the Meditation in the Golden Chamber of Melchizedek beginning on page 34. Share, then do the standard closing. Since it is a holiday, a potluck is recommended, or have the class supply more refreshments than usual and perhaps share small gifts and have a longer social period. As with all the holidays and classes, these ideas are optional, so use your intuition and creativity and feel free to change the format. This is meant only as a tentative structure you can build on or change as you see fit.

Easter

The celebration of this holiday begins with the standard opening for every class as described in chapter 1. The masters recommend adding to this opening process recitations of the Lord's Prayer three times, the Rosary of your choice three times, the prayer of Saint Francis three times and the short version of the Great Invocation once. When this is complete read chapter 4 in *The Complete Ascension Manual*, "Ascension—the 6th Initiation." Also recommended is chapter 12, "Physical Immortality" from *Soul Psychology (Vol. II)*. Choose one of these chapters or read passages from both. Again, have each person take a turn reading aloud, if they want to. When the reading is complete, take time for sharing and questions, then take a 15-minute break.

After the break the masters recommend playing the meditation tape, "Updated God Ascension Seat," or read it, beginning on page 39, which takes about 30 to 40 minutes. Then take time for personal sharing. Because this is a holiday, a potluck or extra refreshments are in order.

Celebrating Thanksgiving

To celebrate this holiday, begin with the standard opening. Then the masters recommend reading chapter 20, "The Laws of Manifestation" in

Soul Psychology (Vol. II) or some of your favorite Psalms from the Old Testament or other inspired writings of choice. Allow sharing and questions during this process. Take 25 minutes for the reading, then for the next 35 minutes go around the circle and let each person share what they have to be grateful about in their life, each taking 2 to 5 minutes. When this is over, take a 15-minute break.

After the break, the masters recommend taking 45 minutes to play the meditation tape called "Ultimate Cosmic Ray Meditation" or read it, beginning on page 31. Then take time for sharing. When this is complete, do the standard closing ceremony. Extra refreshments and/or a potluck before or after class is in order, given the nature of this holiday. This class does not have to be celebrated on the day of Thanksgiving; a day or two before might be a good way to bring in this holiday.

Sai Baba's Birthday

His holiness the Lord Sai Baba is the cosmic Christ for this planet, a universal avatar and the most highly advanced incarnated physical being in the history of the Earth. The masters recommend that lightworkers celebrate his birthday, which is on November 23. Begin this holiday with the standard opening. Sai Baba recommends that you then read chapter 12, "The Cosmic Christ: the Advent of Sathya Sai Baba" in *The Complete Ascension Manual*. If you have other books about him you might be guided to use other texts.

Instead of reading together, you might get one of his video tapes. My favorite is "The Aura of Divinity," about two hours long. Perhaps the Bodhi Tree Bookstore in Los Angeles carries it. (Because of its length you will have to decide how you want to structure the class and celebration.) When you have completed the reading or the video tape, take time for sharing and then take a 15-minute break.

After the break the masters recommend that you chant together the Hindu names of God and the power words from chapter 3. This is even more powerful if the leader of the group first guides a meditation that takes everyone to the love seat of Sai Baba in his inner-plane ashram. In a bilocated state, with eyes physically open, the Hindu mantras could be read aloud while experiencing the love and sweetness of this avatar. Afterward take time for sharing, then do the standard closing. As with all holidays, have some extra refreshments on hand.

If you would like to give your classmates an inexpensive gift on Sai Baba's birthday, you can order by mail passport-size photos of Sai Baba from the Sai Baba bookstore in Tustin, CA (714) 669-0522. (You can have them pick out an assortment. I think they cost about $3 apiece.)

Full Moon Celebrations

We have already talked about three full moon celebrations (Wesak, the Festival of the Christ and the Festival of Humanity) among the thirteen each year. These are the main three that the inner-plane ascended masters recommend that lightworkers celebrate. However, they also recommend honoring the other ten full moons as holy days. Some possible ideas, in terms of how to celebrate these occasions, are as follows:

Begin with the standard opening. The masters recommend adding the long version of the Great Invocation (pp. 4-5). They also recommend the Affirmation of the Disciple (pp. 8-9). When this is complete, the masters have recommended reading chapter 36, "Pan and the Nature Spirits" or chapter 35, "The Angelic Hierarchy," both from *Hidden Mysteries (Vol. II)*.

If it is a warm evening outside, you might consider holding the class outdoors, if that is practical. If not, for perhaps 15 minutes the group can go outside, hold hands and call in the energies of the full moon and the inner-plane ascended masters, for a quiet, receptive meditation. Afterward take time for sharing, then take a 15-minute break. Then the masters recommend the meditation beginning on page 42, the Fifty-Point Cosmic Cleansing Meditation. This should take about 45 minutes. Take time for sharing, then do the standard closing. Have extra refreshments available, since it is a holy day.

Because the full moon allows a greater opening and downpouring of spiritual energies, it is highly recommended that you take advantage of these openings.

7

132 Class Outlines

These potential classes are not put in any specific order. I recommend that the leader(s) of the class put a checkmark next to those you feel intuitively guided to focus on. After checking the class ideas you are most drawn to, then I recommend prioritizing them by your favorites and by the order you want them to unfold.

If this class is leaderless—or, more aptly put, if *everyone* is a leader—you can vote on which subjects the group wants to focus on. My ascension series is so comprehensive that the volumes could supply new classes for four or five years without repeating a subject. The masters urge you to use your own intuition and inner guidance about the subjects to focus on. I have numbered the following 132 class suggestions for easy reference.

Class 1
Removing the Core Fear Matrix

This class, as with all classes, begins with the opening described in chapter 1. Then call forward El Morya, Kuthumi, Serapis Bey, Paul the Venetian, Hilarion, Sananda, Saint Germain, Djwhal Khul and Vywamus to overlight and guide this class during the reading, discussions and meditation that follow.

Ask these inner-plane ascended masters to remove all the core fear they can from each individual and from the group body during and after the reading. Then let the class take turns reading chapter 5, "The Core Fear Matrix Removal Program" in *Beyond Ascension (Vol. III)*. On the audio cassette I guide an even deeper cleansing of core fear and negative-ego programming, among other things. The inner-plane ascended masters will remove the core fear programming, like pulling weeds from a beautiful garden, during your reading and discussion. Reading and talking does not interfere with this process.

Take a 15-minute break after about 45 minutes of reading and discussion.

After the break read the Fifty-Point Cosmic Cleansing Meditation beginning on page 42 to the class members, leaving time between each cleansing activation for the inner-plane ascended masters to do their work.

The advantage of the tape is that the leader can relax and participate in the meditation, too. The fact that it is my voice that guides the meditation may be an advantage to some. You will be doing so many classes that you can rotate between tapes and reading meditations for a change of pace. After the meditation do personal sharing and the closing ceremony. Afterward is socializing, networking and refreshments.

Class 2
Working with the Twelve Planetary Rays

Begin with the standard opening. Then call forth Lord Buddha, Lord Maitreya, Allah Gobi, El Morya, Kuthumi, Serapis Bey, Paul the Venetian, Hilarion, Sananda, Saint Germain, Djwhal Khul, Helios and Vesta, Virgin Mary, Quan Yin, Isis, Lakshmi and Pallas Athena. Ask these beloved masters to overlight and guide the reading of the chapter, the discussion and the later meditation.

Take turns reading chapter 10, "Esoteric Psychology and the Science of the Twelve Rays," in *The Complete Ascension Manual (Vol. I)*. Take time for sharing and discussion.

Take a break. Play the audio-tape meditation, "Ultimate Cosmic Ray Meditation," or lead it, beginning on page 31. Take time for sharing. Do the closing. Social time.

Class 3
The Seven Levels of Initiation

Begin with the standard opening. Call forth Lord Buddha, Lord Maitreya, Allah Gobi, Saint Germain, El Morya, Kuthumi, Serapis Bey, Paul the Venetian, Hilarion, Sananda, Djwhal Khul, Virgin Mary, Quan Yin, Isis, Lakshmi, Helios and Vesta and Pallas Athena.

Take turns reading chapter 1, "The Seven Levels of Initiation," from *Beyond Ascension*. Discuss the material and share.

Take a break. Play the audio tape, "Ultimate Ascension Activation Meditation," or lead the Ascension Meditation and Treatment starting on page 45. Standard closing. Personal sharing time. Social time.

Class 4
Achieving Christ Consciousness

Begin with standard opening. Call forth Sananda, Kuthumi and Lord Maitreya, asking them to take the group in a merkabah to Sananda's ashram and to overlight and guide your reading and discussion.

Read chapter 4, "The Christ Consciousness and How to Achieve It," in *Soul Psychology (Vol. II)*. Discuss how these principles are working in your life.

Take a break. In the second half you can either continue this discussion or listen to the audio tape, "Core Love Meditation," or as an alternative, read the meditation, Invoking a Shower of Core Love and Core Light, beginning on page 75. Ask these three masters to help in this meditation. Take time for sharing afterward. Standard closing ceremony. Social time.

Class 5
Soul Psychology Compared to Traditional Psychology

Start with standard opening. Call forward ascended master Hilarion and ask him to bilocate your group in his group merkabah to his inner-plane ashram during the reading and discussion period. Ask him to overlight and guide the entire session. Read chapter 5, "Soul Psychology as Compared to Traditional Psychology," in *Soul Psychology*. Have a discussion and questions.

Take a break. Continue the discussion during the second half on the value of the two forms of psychology to the whole, and how each is a sliver of truth. Listen to the audio tape, "Ultimate Ascension Activation Meditation," or read Ascension Meditation and Treatment starting on page 45. Ask that Master Hilarion help with all the activations and meditations. Take time for sharing. Do standard closing. Social time.

Class 6
Owning Your Personal Power

Standard opening. Take turns reading chapter 1, "The Development of Personal Power and the Functioning of the Conscious and Subconscious Minds," from *Soul Psychology*. While reading this chapter ask to bilocate to El Morya's inner-plane ashram. Call upon him for guidance and help in your discussion. Conduct a discussion about how everyone either owns their personal power or gives it away to the subconscious mind, negative ego, inner child, emotional body, mental body, physical body, lower-self desire or other people.

Take a break, then set up the audio tape, "Ultimate Cosmic Ray Meditation" or read it, starting on page 31. Ask that El Morya guide the meditation. Personal sharing. Do standard closing. Social time.

Class 7
Integrating the Three Minds and Four Bodies

Standard opening. Call forward Serapis Bey to supply his group merkabah to take you to his inner-plane ashram to sit in his ascension seat, and guide your session and all the later ascension activations and cleansings you will be doing. Read chapter 3, "Integrating the Three Minds and Four Bodies," from *Soul Psychology*. Discuss how the subconscious, conscious and superconscious minds are being balanced in your personal life. Discuss balancing the physical, emotional, mental, spiritual and etheric bodies.

Take a break. Read the Fifty-Point Cosmic Cleansing Meditation starting on page 42. Personal sharing. Standard closing. Social time.

Class 8
Ascension Activation Class

Begin with the standard opening. Then call forth Melchizedek, the Mahatma, Metatron, the seven chohans and Djwhal Khul, asking them to overlight and guide the reading, discussion and meditation. Then read, taking turns, chapter 26, "The Cutting Edge of Ascension: Information and Techniques," from *The Complete Ascension Manual*. As you read each technique, invoke its activation. Take time for discussion and sharing.

Take a break, then lead the Ascension Meditation and Treatment in chapter 27 of the same name in *The Complete Ascension Manual* or beginning on page 45. Take time for sharing, then do standard closing. Social time.

Class 9
How to Reprogram the Subconscious Mind

Standard opening. Call forward the ascended masters Djwhal Khul and Vywamus to supply a group merkabah to take you to Djwhal Khul's inner-plane ashram. Ask them to guide your session, including the ascension activations and reprogramming. Read chapter 10, "How to Reprogram the Subconscious Mind," from *Soul Psychology*. Discuss how the process of reprogramming your own subconscious mind is coming along. What tools do you find most effective? Go through each tool and discuss how each one personally works for you.

Take a break. Next do the "core-fear matrix removal" described in *Beyond Ascension*. Call for this program to be lowered into each individual and the entire group body. Ask the inner-plane ascended masters to first remove all core fear, then all negative ego, all separative thinking, all negative emotions, all negative-ego thought forms, all anger, moodiness, depression, upset, impatience, irritability, grudges and/or any other negative-ego attributes you can think of or have time for. Do each of them for a minute or two, then move on to the next. Save 10 or 15 minutes at the end of the session for the masters to bring forth a downpouring of Core Love, which is filled with the Christ/Buddha attributes, to reprogram the subconscious mind. Leave a few minutes for personal sharing. Do standard closing. Social time.

Class 10
Glamour, Illusion, Maya

Standard opening. Call forward Djwhal Khul to supply his group merkabah to take you to his inner-plane ashram and guide your class and all the ascension activations. Take turns reading chapter 6, "Glamour, Illusion, Maya," from *The Complete Ascension Manual*. Discuss how glamour operates on the emotional plane for each class member, how illusion operates on the mental plane, and how maya operates on the etheric plane.

Take a break. Read the Meditation in the Golden Chamber of Melchizedek beginning on page 34. Personal sharing. Do standard closing. Social time.

Class 11
The Soul, Higher Self or the Oversoul

Standard opening. Call forward Djwhal Khul to supply his group merkabah to take you to his inner-plane ashram and guide the session. Read chapter 9, "The Soul," from *The Complete Ascension Manual*. Discuss each class member's relationship to the higher self and the material in this session.

Take a break. Instead of doing a meditation, break into groups of two or three and have each person call in their higher self (or monad, if they prefer). Have them practice voice-channeling the higher self's overview of how they are doing on their spiritual path. The other person(s) need to ask questions of the higher self about the person's life to stimulate the flow of information. Take turns doing this so that each person has a chance to practice channeling. At the close return to the larger group for personal sharing about the channeling practice. Do standard closing. Social time.

Class 12
Golden Keys to Achieving Ascension in This Lifetime

Standard opening. Call forward Djwhal Khul and Sananda to supply a group merkabah to take you to the inner-plane ashram of Djwhal Khul and guide your session. Read chapter 25, "Golden Keys to Achieving Ascension in This Lifetime," from *The Complete Ascension Manual*. Discuss the keys that were read.

Take a break. Read the meditation, Ascension Meditation and Treatment, beginning on page 45. Personal sharing. Standard closing. Social time.

Class 13
How to Build Your Light and Love Quotient

Standard opening. Call forward Metatron and the divine Mother to guide your session. Read chapter 3, "How to Build Your Light Quotient," from *Beyond Ascension*. Discuss the significance of the light quotient and the thoughts and feelings of group members on the material.

Take a break. Call forward different masters to help build your light quotient. Begin with Archangel Metatron for 5 minutes, then switch to the Ma-

hatma, to Melchizedek, and then to Archangel Michael. Then switch your focus to building the love quotient. Begin by calling in the divine Mother for 5
minutes, then his holiness the Lord Sai Baba. Then call forward the Virgin
Mary, Quan Yin, Isis, Vesta, Lakshmi and Pallas Athena. End the meditation
by calling in the entire Planetary and Cosmic Hierarchy for a 5-minute light
shower, then a 5-minute love shower, then a 5-minute combined love-and-
light shower. Personal sharing. Standard closing. Social time.

Class 14
The Golden Keys to Effective Romantic Relationships

Standard opening. Call forward Kuthumi, Djwhal Khul, Quan Yin, Virgin Mary, Isis, Lakshmi and Vesta to bring forth a group merkabah to take
you to Master Kuthumi's inner-plane ashram, where the class will take
turns reading chapter 12, "The Golden Keys to Effective Romantic Relationships," from *Ascension and Romantic Relationships (Vol XIII)*. Discuss
the material.

Take a break. Play the audio tape, "Ultimate Cosmic Ray Meditation,"
or lead it, beginning on page 31. Personal sharing. Standard closing. Social
time.

Class 15
Working with the Ascension Seats

Begin with the standard opening. Then call forth Melchizedek, the Mahatma, Metatron, Melchior, Helios and Vesta, Lord Buddha, Lord Maitreya
and Saint Germain to overlight and guide this class during the reading, discussion and meditation.

Then take turns reading aloud in turn chapter 2, "Instructions for Utilizing the Planetary and Cosmic Ascension Seats" in *Cosmic Ascension (Vol
VI)*. After reading this section, take time for questions, answers and sharing, then take a break.

After the break play my audio tape, "Updated God Ascension Seat
Meditation," or read it aloud beginning on page 39, pausing about 5 minutes between each ascension seat. Take time for personal sharing after the
meditation. Do the closing, then take social time and have refreshments.

Class 16
Channeling Practice

Begin with the standard opening. Call forth Lord Buddha, Lord Maitreya, Allah Gobi, Saint Germain, El Morya, Kuthumi, Serapis Bey, Paul
the Venetian, Hilarion, Sananda, Djwhal Khul, Virgin Mary, Quan Yin,
Isis, Lakshmi, Helios and Vesta and Pallas Athena.

Take turns reading chapter 18, "Channeling," in *Soul Psychology*, especially the part about how to channel. Take time for discussion and sharing.

Take a break. In the second half there will be no meditation; instead, break into groups of two or three and let each person take a turn at channeling a master of his or her choice. The other members of the smaller groups will ask questions to help facilitate the flow of information. Instruct group members to look at this as a role-playing situation and experiment to avoid feeling foolish. Though it may begin in a type of role-playing, the masters will begin flowing through the role-playing to the point where everyone will be doing intuitive channeling. Asking questions helps keep the process flowing. This channeling practice is the experiential part of the class. Take time afterward to gather and share experiences. Do standard closing. Social time.

Class 17
Mantras, Names of God and Power Words

This class will begin with the standard opening. Call forth Lord Buddha, Lord Maitreya, Allah Gobi, Saint Germain, El Morya, Kuthumi, Serapis Bey, Paul the Venetian, Hilarion, Sananda, Djwhal Khul, Virgin Mary, Quan Yin, Isis, Lakshmi, Helios and Vesta and Pallas Athena.

Read chapter 24, "Mantras, Names of God and Words of Power," in *The Complete Ascension Manual*. Discussion and sharing time. Take a break.

Instead of a formal meditation, chant and recite together all the mantras, names of God and power words I have included in both chapter 3 and in the chapter read in the first part of the class. Spend the second hour of the class reciting in unison, for example, the Egyptian, Hindu, Jewish and Christian mantras. If there's time, go through your favorite ones a second time. Take some silent time between the different religious mantras to attune to that resonance. Sharing time, then the standard closing. Social time and refreshments.

Class 18
God and the Cosmic Hierarchy

Begin with the standard opening. Call forth Melchizedek, the Mahatma, Metatron, the divine Mother, Archangel Michael, Sai Baba, the archangels and the elohim, asking them to overlight, guide and direct your reading, discussion and meditation. Read chapter 17, "God and the Cosmic Hierarchy," in *The Complete Ascension Manual*. Discussion and sharing.

Take a break. Play the meditation tape, "God Ascension Seat Journey," or read the updated God Ascension Seat Meditation starting on page 39. Standard closing. Social time and refreshments.

Class 19
Building the Antakarana

Begin with the standard opening. Call forth the Melchizedek, the Mahatma, Metatron, the divine Mother, Archangel Michael, Sanat Kumara, Lord Buddha, Lord Maitreya, Kuthumi and Djwhal Khul to overlight, guide and direct the reading and discussion that follows, as well as the meditation in the second half. Read chapter 5, "The Building of the Antakarana," in *The Complete Ascension Manual*. Discuss and share.

Take a break. Instead of doing a meditation in the second half, spend the hour doing the techniques in that chapter to build the antakarana: the spiritual vortex, building the central canal, doing the corkscrew meditation, to name a few. Begin the experiential part during the reading in the first hour. When you come to a specific technique for building or expanding the antakarana, stop and do it with the group, calling in the above-mentioned masters to help. Spend the entire class focusing and experiencing these different techniques. Take time to also build the cosmic antakarana, with help from the cosmic masters. Just ask Melchizedek, Mahatma, Metatron, the divine Mother and Archangel Michael to help each class member to build this cosmic antakarana back to Source. "Ask and you shall receive, knock and the door shall be opened." Take time for sharing. Do the closing. Social time and refreshments.

Class 20
Death, Dying and the Science of the Bardo

Begin with the standard opening. Call forth Lord Maitreya, Kuthumi and Djwhal Khul, asking them to provide a group merkabah and bilocate the class to Kuthumi's ashram on the inner plane for the reading and discussion period. Take turns reading chapter 7, "Death, Dying and the Science of the Bardo," in *The Complete Ascension Manual*. Discuss and share.

Take a break. Play the audio meditation, "Ultimate Ascension Activation Meditation," or read Ascension Meditation and Treatment, starting on page 45. Personal sharing. Standard closing. Social time and refreshments.

Class 21
Understanding and Working with your Dreams

Begin with the standard opening. Call forth Lord Buddha, Lord Maitreya, Allah Gobi, Saint Germain, El Morya, Kuthumi, Serapis Bey, Paul the Venetian, Hilarion, Sananda, Djwhal Khul, Virgin Mary, Quan Yin, Isis, Lakshmi, Helios and Vesta and Pallas Athena to provide their group merkabah to take you to Djwhal Khul's inner-plane synthesis ashram for the reading and discussion period. Read chapter 19, "A Spiritual Perspective on Dreams and Sleep," in *Soul Psychology*. Leave time for discussion.

Take a 15-minute break.

After the break, instead of doing a meditation, ask the group to share their night dreams, one person at a time. Then let the group help the dreamer to understand the dream. The inner-plane ascended masters will guide, direct and inspire this discussion. You can talk about important dreams you've had in the past or more recent ones. Do this for the second hour. If people are hesitant to share, then go back to reading a chapter that will stimulate the memory of dreams. Do the standard closing. Social time and refreshments.

Class 22
An Esoteric Understanding of Sexuality

Start with standard opening. Call forward Master Kuthumi to create a group merkabah to take the class to his inner-plane ashram. Ask him to overlight and guide the entire session and help you remain in a bilocated state of consciousness during the reading. Read chapter 13, "An Esoteric Understanding of Sexuality," from *Soul Psychology*. Since this is such personal material, be open to a candid discussion about what you are reading and try to be sensitive to group members. An atmosphere of total unconditional love, support and nonjudgment is always the touchstone.

Take a break. Then listen to the audio tape, "18-Point Cosmic Clearing Meditation," or alternatively, read the Fifty-Point Cosmic Cleansing Meditation beginning on page 42. Ask that Kuthumi guide and direct all the activations and cleansings. Take time for sharing. Do standard closing. Social time.

Class 23
Psychic Self-Defense

Start with standard opening. Call forward ascended master El Morya and Archangel Michael to supply their group merkabah to take you to El Morya's inner-plane ashram and guide your entire session. Taking turns, read chapter 14, "Psychic Self Defense," from *Soul Psychology*. Discuss the material and share.

Take a break. Instead of doing a formal meditation in the second half, practice as a group all the psychic self-defense techniques listed in the chapter so the members can practice them in their daily life. Take time for sharing. Do standard closing. Social time.

Class 24
The Twenty-Two Chakras

Start with standard opening. Call forward Vywamus to supply his group merkabah to take you to his inner-plane ashram and guide the session. Read chapter 16, "The Twenty-Two Chakras," from *Soul Psychology*. Be open to questions and discussion.

Take a break. Then read and guide the group in the meditation, "Ascension Meditation and Treatment," in chapter 27 of *The Complete Ascension Manual* or read it, beginning on page 45. Personal sharing. Do standard closing. Social time.

Class 25
Laws of Manifestation

Standard opening. Call forward Saint Germain to supply his group merkabah to take you to his inner-plane ashram and guide the session, including the manifestation work you will be doing. Read chapter 20, "Laws of Manifestation" in *Soul Psychology*. Discuss how these principles are working in your life.

Take a break. Instead of a formal meditation, pass out paper and pencils and have each person write one Huna prayer, three affirmations, two visualizations and one personal-power action plan. Depending on the size of the group, some of these processes can be shared with the group, then the whole group can perhaps do some together aloud. Another way would be to break into smaller groups of two or three, sharing and vocalizing these different processes. Do closing. Social time.

Class 26
Laws of Karma

Standard opening. Call forward the lords of karma, also known as the Karmic Board, to supply their group merkabah to take you to their inner-plane ashram and guide the session, including the ascension activations and cleansings you will be doing later. Taking turns, read chapter 21, "The Laws of Karma," in *Soul Psychology*. Discuss how karma operates in your personal lives and how grace supersedes it.

Take a break. Set up the audio meditation, "18-Point Cosmic Clearing Meditation," or alternatively, read the Fifty-Point Cosmic Cleansing Meditation beginning on page 42. Standard closing. Personal sharing. Social time.

Class 27
Romantic Relationships from the Soul's Perspective

Standard opening. Call forward Quan Yin to guide the session and the ascension activations. Read chapter 7, "Romantic Relationships from the Soul's Perspective," from *Soul Psychology*. Discuss how romantic relationships and spirituality work together. What is the difference between a personality-level and a spiritual-level romantic relationship? Talk about how your romantic relationship is working or how you would like one to work.

After the break read the Divine Mother and Lady Master's Meditation starting on page 52. Personal sharing. Do standard closing. Social time.

Class 28
Parenting the Inner Child

Standard opening. Call forward the Virgin Mary to supply her group merkabah to take you to her inner-plane ashram and guide your session. Read chapter 2, "Unconditional Self-Love and the Inner Child," in *Soul Psychology*. Discuss the inner child, how it operates in all of your lives, and how it integrates with your conscious mind and higher self.

Take a break. Play the audio tape, "Core Love Meditation," or alternatively, lead the meditation, Invoking a Shower of Core Love and Core Light, beginning on page 75. Personal sharing. Do standard closing. Social time.

Class 29
Hypnosis and Self-Hypnosis

Standard opening. Call forward ascended master Hilarion to supply his group merkabah to take you to his inner-plane ashram and guide the session and the ascension activations. Take turns reading chapter 11, "Hypnosis and Self-Hypnosis," from *Soul Psychology*. Discuss how hypnosis and self-hypnosis operate in your daily lives.

Take a break. If the leader is comfortable leading a guided hypnosis session, this could be the meditation. Hypnosis and meditation are almost the same thing. The only difference is the purpose for which you are using the altered state of consciousness. Another possibility would be to read some kind of guided meditation that is closer to a true hypnosis. If the leader is not comfortable with either of these ideas, then select a meditation of your choice. Personal sharing. Standard closing. Social time.

Class 30
The World's Religions

Standard opening. Call forward the seven chohans to supply their group merkabah to take you to the inner-plane ashram of Sananda and to guide the session and the ascension activations. Read chapter 22, "The Universality of Religion," in *The Complete Ascension Manual*. Discuss.

Take break. Lead the Meditation in the Golden Chamber of Melchizedek beginning on page 34. Personal sharing. Do standard closing. Social time.

Class 31
The Story of Creation

Standard opening. Call forward Melchizedek, the Mahatma and Metatron to supply a group merkabah to take you to Melchizedek's inner-plane ashram to sit in his ascension seat and guide your session and all the ascension activations. Read chapter 1, "The Story of Creation," from *The Complete Ascension Manual*. Discuss the channeled viewpoint of creation as opposed to traditional religion or science.

Take a break. Play the audio tape, "Ultimate Ascension Activation Meditation," or lead the Ascension Meditation and Treatment beginning on page 45. Personal sharing. Do standard closing. Social time.

Class 32
Between Lifetimes

Standard opening. Call forward Lord Buddha, our Planetary Logos, to supply his group merkabah to take you to his inner-plane ashram to sit in his ascension seat and guide your session and ascension activations. Read chapter 8, "Between Lifetimes," from *The Complete Ascension Manual*. Discuss life on the inner plane and class members' thoughts and feelings about the material.

Take a break. Play the audio tape, "God Ascension Seat Journey," or read the updated version beginning on page 39. Personal sharing. Do standard closing. Social time.

Class 33
Lord Buddha and the Planetary Hierarchy

Standard opening. Call forward Lord Buddha and Sanat Kumara to supply a group merkabah to take you to the inner-plane ashram to sit in the ascension seat of Lord Buddha and guide your session and the ascension activations. Take turns reading chapter 16, "Sanat Kumara and the Planetary Hierarchy," from *The Complete Ascension Manual*. Discuss information in the chapter.

Take a break. Play the audio tape, "Ultimate Cosmic Ray Meditation," or read it, beginning on page 31. Personal sharing. Do standard closing. Social time.

Class 34
The Mahatma

Standard opening. Call forward the Mahatma to guide your session. Read chapter 19, "Teachings of Vywamus on the Avatar of Synthesis, the Mahatma," from *The Complete Ascension Manual*. Discuss the nature of the Mahatma and his personal significance.

Take a break. For the meditation begin by calling in the Mahatma and requesting that he fully integrate and merge with each person in the group. Request an ascension activation. Ask the Mahatma to anchor the rods of light and the tones that are appropriate for each person. Then lead the meditation in the Golden Chamber of Melchizedek beginning on page 34. Personal sharing. Standard closing. Social time.

Class 35
The Melchizedek Priesthood

Standard opening. Call forward Melchizedek to supply his group merkabah to take you to his inner-plane ashram to sit in his ascension seat and guide your session. Read chapter 21, "The Melchizedek Priesthood," from *The Complete Ascension Manual*. Discuss the significance of being in the Order of Melchizedek.

Take a break. Read the Meditation in the Golden Chamber of Melchizedek beginning on page 34. Personal sharing. Standard closing. Social time.

Class 36
Prophecies of Things to Come

Standard opening. Call forward Melchizedek, Metatron and the Mahatma to supply a group merkabah to take you to Melchizedek's inner-plane ashram to sit in his ascension seat and guide your session. Read chapter 23, "Prophecies of Things to Come," from *The Complete Ascension Manual*. Let the members discuss their thoughts and feelings about different prophecies.

Take a break. Play the audio tape, "Ultimate Ascension Activation Meditation," or read Ascension Meditation and Treatment beginning on page 45. Personal sharing. Standard closing. Social time.

Class 37
Hermes-Thoth and the Seven Great Universal Laws

Standard opening, Call forward Hermes-Thoth and Buddha to supply a group merkabah to take you to Buddha's inner-plane ashram so you can sit in his ascension seat. Ask them to guide your session. Taking turns, read chapter 21, "Hermes-Thoth and the Seven Great Universal Laws," from *The Ascended Masters Light the Way (Vol. V)*. Discuss the seven Hermetic laws and their significance in your personal life.

Take a break. Play the audio tape, "Ultimate Cosmic Ray Meditation," or read it, beginning on page 31. Personal sharing. Standard closing. Social time.

Class 38
How to Open, Anchor and Activate the Fifty Chakras

Standard opening. Call forward Lord Maitreya, Lord Buddha, Allah Gobi and Saint Germain to supply a group merkabah to take you to Lord Buddha's inner-plane ashram to sit in his ascension seat. Ask them to guide your session. Read chapter 2, "How to Open, Anchor and Activate the Fifty Chakras," from *Beyond Ascension*. Discuss the process of anchoring chakras, opening petals, layers and facets of chakras. Call to the inner-plane ascended masters for the highest possible anchoring and opening of chakras as you read and discuss this material.

Take a break. Read the meditation in the Golden Chamber of Melchizedek beginning on page 34. Personal sharing. Standard closing. Social time.

Class 39
The Seven Paths to Higher Evolution

Standard opening. Call forward Djwhal Khul and Vywamus to supply a group merkabah to take you to Djwhal Khul's inner-plane ashram and guide your session. Read chapter 12, "The Seven Paths to Higher Evolution," from *Beyond Ascension*. Discuss which of the seven paths of higher evolution each class member expects to choose.

Take a break. Play the audio tape, "Ultimate Cosmic Ray Meditation" or read it, beginning on page 31. Personal sharing. Standard closing. Social time.

Class 40
Cosmic Ascension

Standard opening. Call forward the Mahatma to guide your session. Read chapter 15, "Cosmic Ascension," from *Beyond Ascension*. Discuss the profound nature of the cosmic ascension as described in the chapter.

Take a break. Play the audio tape, "God Ascension Seat Journey" or read the updated version beginning on page 39. Personal sharing. Standard closing. Social time.

Class 41
Extraterrestrials and Governmental Cover-ups

Standard opening. First call in the Lord of Arcturus and the Arcturians and Commander Ashtar and the Ashtar Command to overlight this class. Have them build your light quotient while you read chapter 1, "Extraterrestrials and Other Governmental Cover-ups," from *Hidden Mysteries (Vol. IV)*. Discuss the information in the book.

Take a break. Play the audio tape, "Ultimate Ascension Activation Meditation" or read Ascension Meditation and Treatment beginning on page 45. Ask for specific help during this meditation from the Lord of Arcturus and the Arcturians and Commander Ashtar and the Ashtar Command. Personal sharing. Standard closing. Social time.

Class 42
The Hollow Earth

Standard opening. Ask for a golden dome of protection from Archangel Michael for the duration of the session. First, call to the ascended masters of the Hollow Earth to allow you and your classmates to sit in the ascension seat while you read chapter 2, "Agartha in the Hollow Earth," from *Hidden Mysteries*. Discuss the material, aware that you are building your light quotient simultaneously.

Take a break. Read Ascension Meditation and Treatment beginning on page 45 and in chapter 27 of *The Complete Ascension Manual*. Ask the ascended masters of the Hollow Earth to help with the activations during your meditation. Personal sharing. Do standard closing. Social time.

Class 43
The Angelic Hierarchy

Standard opening. Call in the archangels to overlight and guide the session. Read chapter 35, "The Angelic Hierarchy," from *Hidden Mysteries*. Discuss the material in the chapter and members' personal relationships to angels.

Take a break. Read the Divine Mother and Lady Masters Meditation and Activation beginning on page 52. Personal sharing. Standard closing. Social time.

Class 44
Pan and the Nature Spirits

Standard opening. Call in Pan to overlight and guide your session. Read chapter 30, "Pan and the Nature Spirits," from *Hidden Mysteries*. Discuss the material in the chapter and members' personal relationships to Pan and the nature kingdom.

Take a break. Read the Specialized Ascension Activations beginning on page 37. Personal sharing. Standard closing. Social time.

Class 45
Initiation in the Great Pyramid

Standard opening. Call forward Isis, Osiris, Horus, Thoth and Serapis Bey to supply a group merkabah to take the class to Serapis Bey's inner-plane ashram to sit in his ascension seat while you read and discuss chapter 40, "Initiation in the Great Pyramid," from *Hidden Mysteries*. Discuss the material in the chapter.

Take a break. Ask that the class be taken in a group merkabah to the Great Pyramid ascension seat while you read the Ascension Meditation and Treatment beginning on page 45. Personal sharing. Standard closing. Social time.

Class 46
Healing with Color and Sound

Standard opening. Call forward Paul the Venetian to bring forth a group merkabah to take you to his inner-plane ashram. While sitting in Master

Kuthumi's ashram, read chapter 42, "Healing with Color and Sound," from *Hidden Mysteries*. Discuss the material.

Take a break. Have the class do 5 minutes of toning aloud, then play the audio tape, "Ultimate Cosmic Ray Meditation," or read it, beginning on page 31. Personal sharing. Standard closing. Social time.

Class 47
The Twenty-Two Sacred Paths of Yoga

Standard opening, Call forward Sai Baba, Babaji, Paramahansa Yogananda, Rama Krishna, Sri Yukteswar and Swami Sivananda to overlight the class while reading and discussing chapter 46, "The Sacred Paths of Yoga," from *Hidden Mysteries*. Discuss the teachings you are reading about.

Take a break. From the World Service Meditations beginning on page 56, read those that feel appropriate for this time. Personal sharing. Standard closing. Social time.

Class 48
Fundamentalist Christianity and Contamination of Negative Ego

Standard opening. Call forward Sananda and Lord Maitreya to bring forth a group merkabah to take you to Sananda's inner-plane ashram while reading and discussing chapter 48, "The Church's Contamination by Ego," from *Hidden Mysteries*. Discuss the material.

Take a break. Read the Meditation in the Golden Chamber of Melchizedek beginning on page 34. Personal sharing. Standard closing. Social time.

Class 49
The Kabbalistic Tree of Life

Standard opening. Call forward Melchizedek, Metatron and the Mahatma to bring forth a group merkabah to take you to Melchizedek's inner-plane ashram to sit in his ascension seat while reading and discussing chapter 51, "The Kabbalistic Tree of Life," from *Hidden Mysteries*. Discuss the material.

Take a break. Read the Meditation in the Golden Chamber of Melchizedek, beginning on page 34. Personal sharing. Standard closing. Social time.

Class 50
Working with the Huna Prayers

Begin with the standard opening. Then call forward Melchizedek, the Mahatma, Metatron, the divine Mother, Archangel Michael, Sanat Kumara, Lord Buddha, Lord Maitreya, Kuthumi and Djwhal Khul and ask them to overlight and guide the reading, discussion and the Huna prayer practice.

Taking turns, read chapter 11, "Huna Prayers," in *Beyond Ascension*. When you come to those that can apply to your class, read them in unison.

Take a break after about 45 minutes of reading, discussion and practice. After the break take 10 minutes for class members to write out his or her personal Huna prayer on any subject important to them. If you have a fax machine or a copier, make copies of each person's prayer and have the class say them aloud together. Otherwise, separate into groups of two or three and have the small groups read the Huna prayers together.

Another way would be to have the group work together on a Huna prayer that would help the whole group—perhaps for ascension activation or world peace. Each person could be given pen and paper to write it out. It is important to not only read about the Huna prayers, but to practice them. If you have extra time, have the group write out a second Huna prayer with contributions from each person. The number of prayer requests and/or their diversity does not matter. When complete, take time for sharing. Do the standard closing. Social time and refreshments.

Class 51
Working with the Arcturians

Begin with the standard opening. Call forth the Lord of Arcturus and the Arcturian temple workers to overlight and guide this class during the reading, discussion and meditation, exploring the different Arcturian techniques. Read chapter 6, "The Advanced Light Technologies of the Arcturians," in *Beyond Ascension*. Leave time for discussion and sharing. Take a break.

Spend the second hour experiencing the different Arcturian technologies. For example, call forth the Arcturian Joy Machine, the golden cylinder of the Lord of Arcturus to clear negative energy and call for the anchoring of the liquid crystals of the Lord of Arcturus. Ask to experience the Arcturian light chamber, which is their ascension seat and the chamber for physical healing on the mothership. Ask to experience Arcturian light-quotient building. Ask to receive the Arcturian plating system. Ask to be hooked up to the Arcturian computers. Ask the Arcturians to balance all your meridians and chakras, using their advanced computers. Ask to experience the Arcturian prana wind clearing device to clear your etheric system of astral, mental and etheric debris. My suggestion is to spend 5 minutes on each of these advanced Arcturian technologies during the last hour of the class to replace your meditation. Time for personal sharing. Standard closing. Social time and refreshments.

Class 52
Life and Teachings of Mahatma Gandhi

Standard opening. Call forward Sai Baba to supply his group merkabah to take you to his inner-plane ashram and guide the session and the ascension activations. Read chapter 13, "The Life and Teachings of Mahatma Gandhi," from *The Ascended Masters Light the Way*. Discuss violence in self and/or how this operates in our society and how we as lightworkers need to deal with it. Discuss Gandhi's example and how the members relate to it. Discuss social action.

Take a break. Chant Hindu mantras (p. 20) and mantras of other religions. You might consider doing the So Ham meditation: inwardly chant *so* on the inbreath and *ham* on the outbreath. This is the meditation of Sai Baba and Baba Muktananda. Do this meditation for 10 to 15 minutes.

Class 53
Paramahansa Yogananda's Life and Teachings

Standard opening. Call forward Paramahansa Yogananda to guide your session and meditation work. Read chapter 8, "Paramahansa Yogananda and the Self-Realization Fellowship," from *The Ascended Masters Light the Way*. You could also read passages from Yogananda's *Autobiography of a Yogi* and/or *Man's Eternal Quest*. Discussion.

Take a break. Do the Hong Sau meditation, which is similar to the So Ham meditation. On the inbreath inwardly say *hong* and on the outbreath *sau*. Let your breathing guide the meditation; if your breathing is erratic, the *hong sau* will be erratic. If the breathing is slow, the *hong sau* will be slow. If there is very little breathing, then you may be living a spiritual current. Do this meditation for 20 minutes as a group. Then spend 20 minutes inwardly doing the Om meditation. Do the Hindu chants and mantras out loud as a group. Standard closing. Social time.

Class 54
The Life and Teachings of Baba Muktananda

Standard opening. Call forward Baba Muktananda to guide this class. Taking turns, read chapter 15, "Baba Muktananda and the Path of Siddha Yoga," from *The Ascended Masters Light the Way*. Discussion, questions and answers.

Take a break. For a meditation, do the So Ham meditation for about 20 minutes inwardly. Do 10 minutes of Om out loud. Do about 20 minutes of Hindu chants and mantras from chapter 3. Personal sharing. Standard closing. Social time.

Class 55
A Course in Miracles

Standard opening. Call forward Sananda to supply his group merkabah to take you to his inner-plane ashram, to guide the session and the ascension activations. Read passages from the book *A Course in Miracles*. This can be done from the Text, the Teacher's Manual, or the Lesson Book. I recommend using the Teacher's Manual. Discuss.

Take a break. Listen to the audio tape, "Core Love Meditation" or alternatively, lead Invoking a Shower of Core Love and Core Light beginning on page 75. Personal sharing. Standard closing. Social time.

Class 56
The I AM Discourses of Saint Germain

Standard opening. Call forward Saint Germain to supply his group merkabah to take you to his inner-plane ashram and guide the session and the ascension work. Read passages from any one of the 14 volumes of channeled books by Godfré Ray King, collectively titled *The I AM Discourses*. Open one of the books anywhere, almost like a divination. Call in Saint Germain to overlight the process. Read aloud together and then discuss the material. (It is advisable to choose from books 3 through 14, skipping the first two, as they are narratives.)

Take a break. Call forward Saint Germain and ask to go in his group merkabah to sit in the Atomic Accelerator for the next hour while you do the following spiritual work, being sure to return when complete (a leader's responsibility). Below is a list of I AM affirmations and I AM Presence prayers. Have copies of these ready and distribute for the second half. Spend the last hour saying these affirmations and prayers aloud, taking periods of silence to absorb the energies invoked. You also might do a 10- or 15-minute meditation chanting the Om mantra inwardly or outwardly. Personal sharing. Standard closing. Social time.

"I AM" Affirmations

Be still and know I Am God!

I Am God living in this body as [your name].

I Am a fully liberated God living in this body as [your name].

I Am the mighty I Am Presence!

I Am the ascended master [your name].

In the name of the beloved presence of God, who I Am.

By the power of God, who I Am.

The mighty I Am Presence is my real self!

I Am the resurrection and the life.

I Am the truth, the way and the life.

I Am the embodiment of divine love.

I Am the open door which no man can shut.

I Am God in action.

I Am the scepter of dominion, the quenchless flame, the dazzling light and divine perfection made manifest.

I Am the revelation of God.

I Am the baptism of the Holy Spirit.

I Am the ascended being I wish to be now.

I Am the realization of God.

I Am an open door to all revelation.

I Am the light that lights up every room I enter.

I Am the presence of God in action this day.

I Am That I Am.

I Am the eternal liberation from all human imperfection.

I Am a perfect channel and instrument of God.

I Am the presence filling my world with perfection this day.

I Am an invincible body of light.

I Am the light that lights every man that comes into the world.

I Am the victory in the light!

I Am the cosmic flame of cosmic victory

"Mighty I Am Presence" Prayers

Mighty I Am Presence, charge my entire mind, emotions, and body with thy ascended-master consciousness and keep it eternally sustained and all-powerfully active.

Mighty I Am Presence, I call you into action to charge your cosmic flame of cosmic victory into my thoughts, emotions, body and world, and wipe out all else.

Mighty I Am Presence, take out of my feeling world every single thing that seems to obstruct the way and the release of your mighty, intelligent energy to go forth and produce the perfect results I desire.

Mighty I Am Presence, I call you into action to take dominion over my thoughts, feelings, emotions, body, home, world and daily activities. Produce your perfection and hold your dominion.

Mighty I Am Presence, take my love and let it flow in fullness and devotion to thee. Take my hands and let them work incessantly for thee. Take my soul and let it be merged in oneness with thee. Take my mind and thoughts and let them be in tune with thee. Take my everything and let me be an instrument of thy work.

Mighty I Am Presence, take complete control of my being, world and activity. See that I make my ascension in this embodiment, for I Am the resurrection, the truth, and the life. I Am the ascension in the light.

Mighty I Am Presence, charge, intensify and expand your cosmic flame of cosmic victory around me. See that I feel naught but your ascended-master victory.

Mighty I Am Presence, I call you forth to place around me the cosmic armor of the cosmic flame of cosmic victory.

Mighty I Am Presence, I face thy eternal sunrise and receive thy mighty radiance and activity visibly manifest in my experience now.

Mighty I Am Presence, consume and dissolve in me all negative, egotistical qualities, their cause, effect, record and memory, and replace them with the fullness of thy perfected spiritual qualities.

Mighty I Am Presence, come forth and charge my being and world every second of this day and forevermore with ascended-master perfection.

Mighty I Am Presence, charge me so full of divine love that every person, place, condition and thing I contact becomes instantly harmonious and obedient to the I Am Presence.

Mighty I Am Presence, see that this home and environment and all connected with them are governed harmoniously and that all who enter manifest only ascended-master consciousness and activity.

Mighty I Am Presence, fill me with your divine love, power and perfect intelligent direction.

Mighty I Am Presence, charge me and my world with the violet transmuting flame of divine love, which consumes all that is undesirable, and keep me clothed forever with thy almighty perfection.

Mighty I Am Presence, consume in me and my world all doubt, fear, jealousy, pride, resentment, irritation, criticism, condemnation and judgment and their cause, effect, record and memory, replacing them with the fullness of the perfection which thou art, keeping it self-sustained in the ever-expanding light of thy glorious presence.

Mighty I Am Presence, descend into this, thy mind and body.

Take full conscious control this instant of all its activities and hold thy dominion and victory here forever.

Mighty I Am Presence, come forth and charge my being and world with that light and love as of a thousand suns, and crowd my path with showers and showers of mighty I Am Presence. Take complete possession of my attention and fill it entire with thyself.

Mighty I Am Presence, protect me from the human suggestions of the outer world that I may go forth accepting only thy mighty Self and thy perfection forever.

Mighty I Am Presence, move everywhere before me today and do all for me and through me perfectly.

Class 57
The Keys of Enoch

Standard opening. Call forward Metatron, Melchizedek, the Mahatma and ascended master Enoch to supply a group merkabah to take you to the inner-plane ashram to sit in the ascension seat of Melchizedek and guide the session and the ascension activations. Read passages of your choice from *The Keys of Enoch*. This can be done from the glossary or from specific Keys. Discussion, questions and answers.

Take a break, then read the Meditation in the Golden Chamber of Melchizedek beginning on page 34. Personal sharing. Standard closing. Social time.

Class 58
The Urantia Book

Standard opening. Call forward Melchizedek to supply his group merkabah to take you to his inner-plane ashram to sit in his ascension seat. Ask him to guide the session and the ascension activations. Read passages of your choice from *The Urantia Book.* It would be wise for the leader to select some appropriate passages in advance, since it is such a profound book and a little heavy in parts. Discuss the material.

Take a break. Play audio tape of "Updated God Ascension Seat Meditation" or read it, beginning on page 39. Personal sharing. Standard closing. Social time.

Class 59
Babaji, the Yogi Christ

Standard opening. Call forward Babaji to guide and direct your session. Read chapter 13, "Babaji, the Yogi Christ," from *The Complete Ascension Manual.* Discuss Babaji and his mission.

Take a break. For the meditation ask for the group to be taken to the cave of Babaji, asking Babaji for an ascension activation and acceleration. Remain in this bilocated state with eyes open and chant the Hindu mantras beginning on page 20. Close eyes and return to Babaji's cave and do 10 minutes of the Om mantra silently. If time still remains, do the silent So Ham mantra in Babaji's cave. Do standard closing. Social time.

Class 60
The Galactic Core and the Cosmic Masters

Standard opening. Call forward Melchior and the galactic masters to supply a group merkabah to take you to his inner-plane ashram to sit in his ascension seat in the galactic core and guide your session and the ascension activations. Taking turns, read chapter 18, "The Galactic Core and the Cosmic Masters," from *The Complete Ascension Manual*, then discuss the material.

Take a break. Play the audio tape, "God Ascension Seat Journey," or lead the updated version beginning on page 39. Personal sharing. Standard closing. Social time.

Class 61
The Inbreath and Outbreath of Brahma

Standard opening. Call forward Archangel Raphael to guide and direct your session. Read chapter 20, "The Inbreath and Outbreath of Brahma," from *The Complete Ascension Manual*. Discuss this material.

Take a break. Play the audio tape, "God Ascension Seat Journey," or lead the updated version beginning on page 39. Personal sharing. Standard closing. Social time.

Class 62
The Life and Teachings of Buddha

Standard opening. Call forward Lord Buddha to supply a group merkabah, take the group to his inner-plane ashram to sit in his ascension seat and guide your session. Read chapter 16, "The Life and Teachings of Buddha," from *The Ascended Masters Light the Way*. (This chapter could also be read at the Wesak ceremony at the full moon of Taurus.) Discuss how the teachings of Lord Buddha, who is now our Planetary Logos, personally affect each class member.

Take a break. Play the audio tape, "Wesak Ceremony 1998," or lead the meditation beginning on page 81. Personal sharing. Standard closing. Social time.

Class 63
Shirdi Sai Baba

Standard opening. Call forward Sai Baba to supply a group merkabah, take you to his inner-plane ashram to sit in his love seat and guide your session. Read chapter 1, "Shirdi Sai Baba," from *The Ascended Masters Light the Way*. Discuss the triple avatar incarnation of his holiness the Lord Sai Baba. Discuss also thoughts and feelings of class members about Sai Baba's incarnation.

Take a break. If by chance you have audio tapes of Sai Baba bajans in English, you could play and sing along with them for 10 to 15 minutes. [These can be ordered in English and Hindi from the Sai Baba bookstore by calling: (714) 669-0522.] Then ask to be taken to his love seat on the inner plane. Ask to be showered with vibhuti ash by Sai Baba. Sit quietly and bask in this for five minutes. Then request to Sai Baba to be bathed in his divine amrita or divine nectar. Bathe in this for 5 minutes. Bathe in the energies of the love seat for 5 minutes, then ask Sai Baba for an ascension activation for each member of the group. Soak this in for another 10 minutes or so. While remaining in the love seat, do 5 to 10 minutes of Om out loud. Then do 10 minutes of the So Ham meditation in accordance with each person's individual inner breathing. Chant out loud the Hindu mantras beginning on page 20 or in *The Complete Ascension Manual*, then return. Personal sharing. Standard closing. Social time.

Class 64
Quan Yin, Bodhisattva of Compassion and Mercy

Standard opening. Call forward Quan Yin to guide your session. Read chapter 17, "Quan Yin, Bodhisattva of Compassion and Mercy," from *The Ascended Masters Light the Way*. Discuss Quan Yin and each person's feeling relationship with this beautiful goddess and ascended lady master.

Take a break. Play the audio tape, "The Divine Mother and Lady Masters Ascension Activation Meditation" or lead it, starting on page 52. Personal sharing. Standard closing. Social time.

Class 65
The Virgin Mary

Standard opening. Call in the Virgin Mary prior to beginning of class. Take turns reading chapter 30, "Appearances and Teachings of the Virgin Mary," from *The Ascended Masters Light the Way*. Discuss the appearances and personal significance of the Virgin Mary.

Take a break. Instead of a formal meditation, this meditation will be the New Age Rosary and the Traditional Rosary beginning on page 6 and also in *The Complete Ascension Manual* (pp. 260-261). After each rosary, sit quietly for five minutes and soak in the energy, then begin the next. Do this for the 45- to 50-minute meditation. An alternate possibility is to do a small number of rosaries, then have the leader read the Divine Mother and Lady Master Meditation beginning on page 52. If you choose the latter, ask the Virgin Mary to help guide and direct all the ascension activations. Personal sharing. Standard closing. Social time.

Class 66
Madam Blavatsky and the Theosophical Society

Standard opening. Call forward ascended masters Lady Helena, Kuthumi, El Morya, Saint Germain and Djwhal Khul to guide your session. Read chapter 33, "Madam Blavatsky and the Theosophical Society," from *The Ascended Masters Light the Way*. Discuss Madam Blavatsky and the significance of the Theosophical Society being given the first dispensation of ascended-master teachings.

Take a break. Play the audio tape, "Ultimate Cosmic Ray Meditation," or read it, beginning on page 31. Personal sharing. Standard closing. Social time.

Class 67
The Sleeping Prophet: Edgar Cayce

Standard opening. Call in the Universal Mind to overlight this class as well as Edgar Cayce himself. Read chapter 38, "The Sleeping Prophet: Edgar Cayce," from *The Ascended Masters Light the Way*. As an alternative, the leader might consider reading from some of the many books written about Cayce. Discuss the chapter and/or his channeling.

Take a break. Play the audio tape, "Ultimate Ascension Activation Meditation" or read the Ascension Meditation and Treatment beginning on page 45. Ask Universal Mind to assist with all the ascension activations in this meditation. Personal sharing. Standard closing. Social time.

Class 68
Saint Germain

Standard opening. Call forward Saint Germain to supply a group merkabah to take you to the atomic accelerator ascension seat and guide your session. Taking turns, read chapter 37, "Count Saint Germain—the 'Wonder Man' of Europe," from *The Ascended Masters Light the Way*. Alternatively, read sections from *The I AM Discourses* by Godfré Ray King. Discuss the significance of Saint Germain and his teachings.

Take a break. Play the audio tape, "Ultimate Cosmic Ray Meditation," or read it, beginning on page 31. Personal sharing. Standard closing. Social time.

Class 69
The Golden Key to Accelerating Your Spiritual Evolution

Standard opening. Call forward Djwhal Khul and Sananda to supply a group merkabah to take you to Djwhal Khul's inner-plane ashram and guide your session. Read chapter 7, "The Golden Key to Accelerating Your Spiritual Evolution," from *Beyond Ascension*. Discuss the significance of the teachings of this chapter both theoretically and personally.

Take a break. Play the audio tape, "Ultimate Ascension Activation Meditation" or read the Ascension Meditation and Treatment beginning on page 45. Personal sharing. Standard closing. Social time.

Class 70
The Twenty-Four Dimensions of Reality

Standard opening. Call forward Vywamus to guide your session. Read chapter 10, "The Twenty-Four Dimensions of Reality," from *Beyond Ascension*. Discuss the nature of the 24 dimensions of reality.

Take a break. Play the audio tape, "God Ascension Seat Journey" or read the updated version beginning on page 39. Personal sharing. Standard closing. Social time.

Class 71
The Ashtar Command

Standard opening. Call forward Commander Ashtar and the Ashtar Command to overlight and guide this session. Ask Commander Ashtar to supply a merkabah to take the class to his mothership and sit in his ascension seat. Then read and discuss chapter 11, "The Ashtar Command," from *Hidden Mysteries*.

Take a break. Play the audio meditation, "The Ultimate Ascension Activation Meditation," or read the Ascension Meditation and Treatment beginning on page 45, asking Commander Ashtar and the Ashtar Command to supervise the activations. Personal sharing. Standard closing. Social time.

Class 72
The Huna Teachings

Standard opening. Call in Master Kuthumi and Djwhal Khul to bring forth their group merkabah to take you to Master Kuthumi's inner-plane ashram and overlight the session. Take turns reading chapter 3, "Huna Teachings," from *Hidden Mysteries*. Discuss the material.

Take a break. Read the meditations appropriate for the evening from the World Service Meditations beginning on page 56. Personal sharing. Standard closing. Social time.

Class 73
The Science of Soul Travel

Standard opening. Call forward the seven chohans to overlight and guide the session. Taking turns, read chapter 41, "The Science of Soul Travel," from *Hidden Mysteries*. Discuss the material and personal experiences.

Take a break. The meditation will be to practice experientially the soul-travel techniques you have just read about. Ask Archangel Michael and the seven chohans to guide, protect and help you in these practice sessions. Personal sharing. Standard closing. Social time.

Class 74
Brahma, Vishnu and Shiva

Standard opening. Call forward Sai Baba, Paramahansa Yogananda, Babaji, Brahma, Vishnu and Shiva to overlight and guide the session. Call forward Master Kuthumi to bring forth a group merkabah to take you to his inner-plane ashram. Read chapter 43, "Brahma, Vishnu and Shiva," from *Hidden Mysteries*. Discuss the material.

Take a break. Have the class do 15 minutes of Hindu mantras and chants on pages 20-22. Then do 10 minutes of the Om meditation, 15 minutes of the silent So Ham meditation and 10 minutes of the Hong Sau meditation, as described in classes 52-54. Personal sharing. Standard closing. Social time.

Class 75
The Egyptian Mysteries

Standard opening. Call forward Isis, Osiris, Horus, Thoth and Serapis Bey to supply a group merkabah to take the class to Serapis Bey's inner-plane ashram to sit in his ascension seat. Ask them to overlight the session, then read chapter 39, "The Egyptian Mysteries," from *Hidden Mysteries*. Discuss the material.

Take a break. Lead the Specialized Ascension Activations beginning on page 37. Personal sharing. Standard closing. Social time.

Class 76
The *Bhagavad-Gita*

Standard opening. Call forward Sai Baba and Krishna to bring forth a group merkabah to take you to his inner-plane ashram to sit in his love seat during the session. Ask them to overlight the session. Take turns reading chapter 44, "The *Bhagavad-Gita*," from *Hidden Mysteries*. Discuss the teachings.

Take a break. Read from the World Service Meditations beginning on page 56 those that feel appropriate for this time. Afterward have the class return. Personal sharing. Standard closing. Social time.

Class 77
The Yoga Sutras of Patanjali

Standard opening. Call forward Djwhal Khul, Sai Baba and Patanjali to bring forth their group merkabah to take you to Djwhal Khul's inner-plane ashram and guide the session. Read chapter 47, "The Yoga Sutras of Patanjali," from *Hidden Mysteries*. Discuss the teachings.

Take a break. Play the meditation tape, "Ultimate Ascension Activation Meditation," or lead the Ascension Meditation and Treatment beginning on page 45. Take time for personal sharing. Standard closing. Social time.

Class 78
The Vedas: God's Revelation

Standard opening. Call forward Sai Baba, Babaji, Paramahansa Yogananda, Rama Krishna and Sri Yukteswar to overlight the session. Then take turns reading chapter 45, "The Vedas: God's Revelation," from *Hidden Mysteries*. Discuss the teachings.

Take a break. Have the class do 15 minutes of Hindu mantras and chants found on pages 20-22. Also do 10 minutes of the Om meditation, then 15 minutes of the silent So Ham meditation and 10 minutes of the Hong Sau meditation (see classes 52-54). Personal sharing. Standard closing. Social time.

Class 79
The Essene Brotherhood

Standard opening. Call forward Sananda and Lord Maitreya to bring forth a group merkabah to take you to Sananda's inner-plane ashram. Ask them to guide the session, then read chapter 50, "The Essene Brotherhood," from *Hidden Mysteries*. Discuss the material.

Take a break. Play the meditation tape, "God Ascension Seat Journey," or lead the updated version beginning on page 39. Personal sharing. Standard closing. Social time.

––––––––––––––––––––––––––––––

[Note: Hereafter are referenced two volumes (*How to Clear the Negative Ego* and *Integrated Ascension: Revelation for the Next Millennium*) that we expect to be published later but that are meanwhile available in manuscript form from the Melchizedek Light Synthesis Academy & Ashram (see the end pages for address).]

––––––––––––––––––––––––––––––

Class 80
Clearing Negative Implants and Negative Elementals

Begin with the standard opening. Call forth Melchizedek, the Mahatma, Metatron, the divine Mother, Archangel Michael, Sai Baba, Lord Buddha, Lord Maitreya, Allah Gobi, El Morya, Kuthumi, Serapis Bey, Paul the Venetian, Hilarion, Sananda, Saint Germain, Djwhal Khul, Helios and Vesta, Virgin Mary, Quan Yin, Isis, Lakshmi and Pallas Athena to guide and overlight the session.

Taking turns, read the chapter, "How to Clear Alien Implants, Elementals and Astral Entities," from *How to Clear the Negative Ego*. Discuss and share.

Take a break. Play the audio meditation, "18-Point Cosmic Clearing Meditation," or alternatively, lead the Fifty-Point Cosmic Cleansing Meditation starting on page 42. Personal sharing time. Standard closing. Social time.

Class 81
Clearing Negative Ego through the Archetypes

Standard opening. Call Sananda, Saint Germain, El Morya, Kuthumi and Djwhal Khul to bring forth a group merkabah to take you to Sananda's inner-plane ashram. Ask them to guide the session. Read and discuss the chapter, "How to Clear Negative Ego through the Archetypes," from *How to Clear the Negative Ego*. Discuss the material.

Take a break. Play the audio tape, "18-Point Cosmic Clearing Meditation" or alternatively, lead the Fifty-Point Cosmic Cleansing Meditation beginning on page 42. Personal sharing. Standard closing. Social time.

Class 82
Clearing Negative Ego through Developing a Healthy Psychoepistemology

Standard opening. Call forth Melchizedek, the Mahatma and Metatron to bring forth a group merkabah to take you to Melchizedek's inner-plane ashram to sit in his ascension seat. Ask them to guide and overlight the session. Taking turns, read the chapter, "Clearing Negative Ego through Developing a Healthy Psychoepistemology," from *How to Clear the Negative Ego*. Discuss the material.

Take a break. Lead the Meditation in the Golden Chamber of Melchizedek beginning on page 34. Personal sharing. Standard closing. Social time.

Class 83
The Fifteen Major Tests of the Spiritual Path

Standard opening. Call forward Lord Buddha, Lord Maitreya, Allah Gobi and Saint Germain to bring forth a group merkabah to take the class to

Lord Buddha's inner-plane ashram to sit in his ascension seat. Ask them to guide the session, then read the chapter, "The Fifteen Major Tests of the Spiritual Path," from *How to Clear the Negative Ego*. Discuss the material.

Take a break. Read the meditations that feel appropriate for this class from the World Service Meditations that begin on page 56. Personal sharing. Standard closing. Social time.

Class 84
The Planetary Ascended Masters and Their Divine Puzzle Pieces

Standard opening. Call forward Lord Maitreya, the seven chohans and Djwhal Khul to bring forth a group merkabah to take the class to Lord Maitreya's inner-plane ashram. Ask them to guide the session, then read chapter 3, "The Planetary Ascended Masters and Their Divine Puzzle Pieces," from *Your Ascension Mission: Embracing Your Puzzle Piece (Vol. X)*. Discuss the material.

Take a break. Play the meditation tape, "Ultimate Cosmic Ray Meditation," or lead it, beginning on page 31. Personal sharing. Standard closing. Social time.

Class 85
What Is Cosmic Ascension?

Standard opening. Call forward Melchizedek, the Mahatma and Metatron to bring forth a group merkabah to take the class to Melchizedek's inner-plane ashram to sit in his ascension seat. Ask them to guide the session, then read chapter 7, "What Is Cosmic Ascension?," from *Cosmic Ascension: Your Cosmic Map Home*. Discuss the material.

Take a break. Play the audio-tape meditation, "God Ascension Seat Journey," or lead the updated version beginning on page 39. Personal sharing. Standard closing. Social time.

Class 86
The Cosmic Rays

Standard opening. Call forward the Lord of Sirius, Vywamus and the Lord of Arcturus to bring forth a group merkabah to take the class to the Lord of Sirius' inner-plane ashram to sit in his ascension seat. Ask them to overlight the session, then take turns reading chapter 3, "The Cosmic Rays," from *Cosmic Ascension: Your Cosmic Map Home*. Discuss the material.

Take a break. Play the audio-tape meditation, "Ultimate Cosmic Ray Meditation," or read it, beginning on page 31. Personal sharing. Standard closing. Social time.

Class 87
How to Use Planetary and Cosmic Ascension Seats

Standard opening. Call forward Melchior, the Lord of Sirius, Vywamus, Sanat Kumara, the Lord of Arcturus and Lenduce to bring forth a group merkabah to take the class to Melchior's inner-plane ashram to sit in his ascension seat. Ask them to guide the session, then read chapter 2, "Instructions for Utilizing Planetary and Cosmic Ascension Seats," from *Cosmic Ascension: Your Cosmic Map Home*. Discuss the material.

Take a break. Play the audio tape, "Updated God Ascension Seat Meditation," or lead it, beginning on page 39. Personal sharing. Standard closing. Social time.

Class 88
Self-Realization and the Issue of Accountability

Standard opening. Call forward El Morya, Djwhal Khul, Saint Germain and Allah Gobi to bring forth a group merkabah to take the class to El Morya's inner-plane ashram. Ask them to guide the session, then read chapter 8, "Self-Realization and the Issue of Accountability," from *Cosmic Ascension: Your Cosmic Map Home*. Discuss the material.

Take a break. Play the audio tape, "Ultimate Ascension Activation Meditation," or lead the Ascension Meditation and Treatment beginning on page 45. Take time for personal sharing. Standard closing. Social time.

Class 89
Spiritual Leadership and Planetary World Service

Standard opening. Call forward Allah Gobi, Lord Maitreya, Kuthumi, Saint Germain and Lord Buddha to bring forth a group merkabah to take the class to Allah Gobi's inner-plane ashram. Ask them to overlight the session. Then take turns reading chapter 9, "Spiritual Leadership and World Service," from *Cosmic Ascension: Your Cosmic Map Home*. Discuss the material.

Take a break. Lead the appropriate meditations from the World Service Meditations beginning on page 56. Personal sharing. Standard closing. Social time.

Class 90
Eighteen Great Cosmic Clearings

Standard opening. Call forward Hilarion and Djwhal Khul to bring forth a group merkabah to take the class to Hilarion's inner-plane ashram. Ask them to guide the session. Read chapter 17, "Eighteen Great Cosmic Clearings," from *Cosmic Ascension: Your Cosmic Map Home*. Discuss the material.

Take a break. Play the audio tape, "18-Point Cosmic Clearing Meditation," or alternatively, lead the Fifty-Point Cosmic Cleansing Meditation beginning on page 42. Personal sharing. Standard closing. Social time.

Class 91
Integrated Ascension

Standard opening. Call forward Melchizedek, the Mahatma, Metatron and Djwhal Khul to bring forth a group merkabah to take the class to Melchizedek's inner-plane ashram to sit in his ascension seat. Ask them to guide the session. Take turns reading the chapter, "Integrated Ascension" from *Integrated Ascension: Revelation for the Next Millennium.* Discuss the material and how it relates to you personally.

Take a break. Lead the Meditation in the Golden Chamber of Melchizedek beginning on page 34. Personal sharing. Standard closing. Social time.

Class 92
Transcending Negative-Ego Archetypal Dualities

Standard opening. Call forward Sananda, Kuthumi, El Morya, Saint Germain, Serapis Bey, Paul the Venetian, Hilarion, Lord Maitreya, Lord Buddha, Allah Gobi, Melchizedek, the Mahatma, Metatron and Djwhal Khul to bring forth a group merkabah to take the class to Sananda's inner-plane ashram. Ask them to guide the session. Then take turns reading the chapter, "Transcending Negative-Ego Archetypal Dualities," from *Integrated Ascension: Revelation for the Next Millennium.* Discuss the material and how it relates to you personally.

Take a break. Lead the Fifty-Point Cosmic Cleansing Meditation" beginning on page 42. Personal sharing. Standard closing. Social time.

Class 93
Dr. Lorphan's Healing Academy on Sirius

Standard opening. Call forward Dr. Lorphan, the galactic healers, Archangel Raphael, the healing angels and Mother Mary to overlight and guide the session. Read the chapter, "Dr. Lorphan's Healing Academy on Sirius," from *Integrated Ascension: Revelation for the Next Millennium.* Discuss the material.

Take a break. The meditation for this class will be to practice the healing tools I have outlined in the second half of the above chapter. Go through them one by one, taking 2 to 3 minutes or longer to experience them in silence. Personal sharing. Standard closing. Social time.

Class 94
Developing an Optimal Physical, Psychological and Spiritual Immune System

Standard opening. Call forward Hilarion, Serapis Bey, Melchizedek, the Mahatma, Metatron and Djwhal Khul to bring forth a group merkabah to take the class to Hilarion's inner-plane ashram. Ask them to guide the session. Take turns reading the chapter, "Developing an Optimal Physical,

Psychological and Spiritual Immune System," from *Integrated Ascension: Revelation for the Next Millennium*. Discuss the material.

Take a break. Play the audio tape, "18-Point Cosmic Clearing Meditation" or alternatively, lead the Fifty-Point Cosmic Cleansing Meditation beginning on page 42. Personal sharing. Standard closing. Social time.

Class 95
Developing a Proper Relationship to the Inner Senses

Standard opening. Call forward Lord Maitreya, Kuthumi and Djwhal Khul to bring forth a group merkabah to take the class to Lord Maitreya's inner-plane ashram. Ask them to overlight the session, then read the chapter, "Integrated Ascension and Developing a Proper Relationship to the Inner Senses," from *Integrated Ascension: Revelation for the Next Millennium*. Discuss the material.

Take a break. Play the audio tape, "Ultimate Ascension Activation Meditation," or lead the Ascension Meditation and Treatment beginning on page 45. Personal sharing. Standard closing. Social time.

Class 96
An Overview on Nonintegrated Ascension

Standard opening. Call forward Kuthumi, Lord Maitreya, Djwhal Khul and the Mahatma to bring forth a group merkabah to take the class to Kuthumi's inner-plane ashram. Ask them to overlight and guide the session, then read the chapter, "An Overview on Nonintegrated Ascension," from the manuscript *Integrated Ascension: Revelation for the Next Millennium*. Discuss the material.

Take a break. Play the audio tape, "Ultimate Cosmic Ray Meditation," or lead it, beginning on page 31. Personal sharing. Standard closing. Social time.

Class 97
Twilight Masters, Cults and Nonintegrated Ascension Groups

Standard opening. Call forward Lord Michael, the divine Mother, Melchizedek, the Mahatma and Metatron to bring forth a group merkabah to take the class to Melchizedek's inner-plane ashram to sit in his ascension seat. Ask them to overlight the session, then take turns reading the chapter, "Twilight Masters, Cults and Non-Integrated Ascension Groups," from *Integrated Ascension: Revelation for the Next Millennium*. Discuss the material.

Take a break. Lead the Meditation in the Golden Chamber of Melchizedek beginning on page 34. Personal sharing. Standard closing. Social time.

Class 98
Ascension in the Many Kingdoms of God

Standard opening. Call forward Lord Buddha, Pan, the elohim councils, Metatron, the archangels and Djwhal Khul to bring forth a group merkabah to take the class to Lord Buddha's inner-plane ashram to sit in his ascension seat. Ask them to guide the session, then read the chapter, "Ascension in the Many Kingdoms of God," from *Integrated Ascension: Revelation for the Next Millennium*. Discuss the material.

Take a break. Lead the meditation, Ascension Meditation and Treatment beginning on page 45. Personal sharing. Standard closing. Social time.

Class 99
Deeper Explanation of the Eight Quotients and How to Use Them

Standard opening. Call forward Djwhal Khul, the seven chohans, Lord Maitreya, Allah Gobi, Saint Germain, Lord Buddha, Helios and Vesta, the Lady Masters, Melchizedek, Metatron and the Mahatma to bring forth a group merkabah to take the class to Djwhal Khul's inner-plane ashram. Ask them to guide the session. Read the chapter, "A Deeper Explanation of the Eight Quotients and How to Use Them," from *Integrated Ascension: Revelation for the Next Millennium*. Discuss the material.

Take a break. Supply each class member with paper and pencil. For the next activity, break up into small groups. Each class member will intuitively estimate, on a scale of 1 to 100, what percentage he or she holds in each of these eight major categories. After completion discuss why they gave themselves that score and what they need to do to improve it—without judging themselves. This discussion will substitute for the meditation. Standard closing. Social time.

Class 100
Seeing Life through a Single Lens Rather Than a Full-Spectrum Perspective

Standard opening. Call forward Melchizedek, Metatron, the Mahatma, Archangel Michael and the divine Mother to bring forth a group merkabah to take the class to Melchizedek's inner-plane ashram to sit in his ascension seat. Ask for overlighting and guidance, then read the chapter, "Seeing Life through a Single Lens Rather Than a Full-Spectrum Perspective," from *Integrated Ascension: Revelation for the Next Millennium*. Discuss the material.

Take a break. Play the audio tape, "Updated God Ascension Seat Meditation," or lead it, beginning on page 39. Personal sharing. Standard closing. Social time.

Class 101
Integrating the Seven Rays and Ray Types

Standard opening. Call forward Lord Maitreya, Lord Buddha, El Morya, Kuthumi, Serapis Bey, Paul the Venetian, Hilarion, Sananda, Saint Germain, Djwhal Khul and the Mahatma to bring forth a group merkabah to take the class to Lord Maitreya's inner-plane ashram. Take turns reading the chapter, "Integrating the Seven Rays and Ray Types," from *Integrated Ascension: Revelation for the Next Millennium*. Discuss the material.

Take a break. Play the audio tape, "Ultimate Cosmic Ray Meditation," or lead it, beginning on page 31. Personal sharing. Standard closing. Social time.

Class 102
Channeling Your Subquotient Scores

Standard opening. Call forward Melchizedek, the Mahatma, Metatron, the divine Mother, Virgin Mary, Quan Yin, Isis, Lakshmi, Vesta, Pallas Athena, El Morya, Kuthumi, Serapis Bey, Paul the Venetian, Hilarion, Sananda, Saint Germain and Djwhal Khul to overlight the session. Read the chapter, "Subquotients," from *Integrated Ascension: Revelation for the Next Millennium*. Discuss the material.

Take a break. Supply pencil and paper to the class members so they can give themselves an intuitive score on each of the subquotients mentioned in the reading, on a scale of 1 to 100. Emphasize that there should be no judgment, just honest, loving evaluation of self about the qualities that are focused on. Afterward break into small groups in which the members can discuss their scores, what they can do to improve and how they can support one another in this process. Standard closing. Social time.

Class 103
Clearing Negative Ego through the Rays

Standard opening. Call forth Hilarion, Serapis Bey, Paul the Venetian, Sananda, Saint Germain, El Morya, Kuthumi and Djwhal Khul to bring forth a group merkabah to take you to Hilarion's inner-plane ashram. Ask them for their guidance in the session. Read the chapter, "Clearing Negative Ego through the Rays," from *How to Clear the Negative Ego*. Discuss the material.

Take a break. Play the audio tape, "Ultimate Cosmic Ray Meditation," or lead it, beginning on page 31. Personal sharing. Standard closing. Social time.

Class 104
Clearing Specific Diseases

Standard opening. Call forward El Morya, Hilarion, Serapis Bey, Paul the Venetian, Sananda, Saint Germain, Kuthumi and Djwhal Khul to bring forth a group merkabah to take you to El Morya's inner-plane ashram. Ask for their guidance, then read the chapter, "Clearing Specific Diseases from the Perspective of the Masters," from *How to Clear the Negative Ego*. Discuss the material.

Take a break. Lead the Fifty-Point Cosmic Cleansing Meditation beginning on page 42. Personal sharing. Standard closing. Social time.

Class 105
Psychological Causation of Disease

Standard opening. Call forward Djwhal Khul to bring forth a group merkabah to take the class to his inner-plane ashram. Ask him to guide the session, then take turns reading the chapter, "Psychological Causation of Disease by Djwhal Khul," from *How to Clear the Negative Ego*. Discuss the material.

Take a break. Play the audio tape, "18-Point Cosmic Clearing Meditation," or alternatively, lead the Fifty-Point Cosmic Cleansing Meditation beginning on page 42. Personal sharing. Standard closing. Social time.

Class 106
The Search for Your Puzzle Piece

Standard opening. Call forward Djwhal Khul and Kuthumi to bring forth a group merkabah to take the class to Djwhal Khul's inner-plane ashram. Ask for their guidance, then read chapter 1, "The Search for Your Puzzle Piece," from *Your Ascension Mission: Embracing Your Puzzle Piece*. Discuss the material.

Take a break. Lead the meditations that feel appropriate from the World Service Meditations beginning on page 56. Personal sharing. Standard closing. Social time.

Class 107
Clearing Negative Ego through the Tree of Life

Standard opening. Call forward Melchizedek, Metatron, the Mahatma, divine Mother and Archangel Michael to bring forth a group merkabah to take the class to Melchizedek's inner-plane ashram to sit in his ascension seat. Ask for their guidance. Read the chapter, "Clearing the Negative Ego through the Tree of Life," from *How to Clear the Negative Ego*. Discuss this material.

Take a break. Read the Meditation in the Golden Chamber of Melchizedek beginning on page 34. Personal sharing. Standard closing. Social time.

Class 108
The Transcendence of Negative Ego
and the Science of the Bardo

Standard opening. Call forward Melchizedek, Metatron, the Mahatma, divine Mother and Archangel Michael to bring forth a group merkabah to take the class to Melchizedek's inner-plane ashram to sit in his ascension seat. Ask them to guide the session, then take turns reading the chapter, "The Transcendence of Negative Ego and the Science of the Bardo," from *How to Clear the Negative Ego*. Discuss the material.

Take a break. Lead the Fifty-Point Cosmic Cleansing Meditation beginning on page 42. Personal sharing. Standard closing. Social time.

Class 109
The Glamour of Ascension

Standard opening. Call forward El Morya, Saint Germain and Djwhal Khul to bring forth a group merkabah to take the class to El Morya's inner-plane ashram. Ask for their guidance, then read chapter 8, "Your Glorious Ascension and Ascension Mission versus the Glamour of Ascension," from *Your Ascension Mission: Embracing Your Puzzle Piece*. Discuss the material.

Take a break. Lead the Fifty-Point Cosmic Cleansing Meditation beginning on page 42. Personal sharing. Standard closing. Social time.

Class 110
Cosmic Evolution and the Mapping of the Higher Mind

Standard opening. Call forward Melchizedek and Metatron to bring forth a group merkabah to take the class to the Melchizedek's inner-plane ashram and sit in his ascension seat. Ask them to guide the session, then take turns reading chapter 4, "Cosmic Evolution and the Mapping of the Higher Mind," from *Cosmic Ascension: Your Cosmic Map Home*. Discuss the material.

Take a break. Play the audio tape, "Ultimate Ascension Activation Meditation," or lead the Ascension Meditation and Treatment beginning on page 45. Personal sharing. Standard closing. Social time.

Class 111
A Cosmic Day and a Cosmic Night

Standard opening. Call forward Lenduce, Vywamus and Sanat Kumara to bring forth a group merkabah to take the class to the Lenduce's inner-plane ashram and sit in his ascension seat. Ask for their guidance, then read chapter 5, "A Cosmic Day and a Cosmic Night," from *Cosmic Ascension: Your Cosmic Map Home*. Discuss the material.

Take a break. Lead the meditations appropriate for the moment from the World Service Meditations beginning on page 56. Personal sharing. Standard closing. Social time.

Class 112
Ultimate Monadic Ascension: The Next Step

Standard opening. Call forward each person's individual monad and mighty I Am Presence and ask them to overlight and guide the session. Take turns reading chapter 6, "Ultimate Monadic Ascension: The Next Step," from *Cosmic Ascension: Your Cosmic Map Home*. Discuss the material.

Take a break. Read Ascension Meditation and Treatment beginning on page 45. Personal sharing. Standard closing. Social time.

Class 113
Integrating and Cleansing One's 144 Soul Extensions

Standard opening. Call forward Lord Buddha, Sanat Kumara and Melchizedek to bring forth a group merkabah to take the class to the Lord Buddha's inner-plane ashram and sit in his ascension seat. Ask for their guidance, then take turns reading chapter 7, "The Importance of Integrating One's 144 Soul Extensions," from *Cosmic Ascension: Your Cosmic Map Home*. Discuss the material.

Take a break. Guide a meditation, first instructing group members to close their eyes and visualize a large round table and the eleven other soul extensions of their oversoul or higher self seated around it with them. Guide them to have a discussion with these soul extensions about working together for the good of the oversoul and monad, or Mighty I Am Presence. Give them at least 5 to 10 minutes.

Afterward, guide the class to move to a higher level and do the same thing with the other 143 soul extensions of the monad. The idea here is to form a partnership and develop a spirit of camaraderie. Give them another 5 to 10 minutes to do this, asking for help from the oversoul and monad. Then call to Lord Buddha, Sanat Kumara and Melchizedek to help cleanse as many soul extensions as possible during this meditation and class time. Then sit in silence for 10 minutes while this work is going on.

If time permits, call for a cleansing of each person's monad and karma to the highest potential. When this is complete, call for a cleansing for each person all the way back to his or her original covenant with God. Take another 10 minutes while this purification takes place. If time permits, do personal sharing. Standard closing. Social time.

Class 114
Comparative Overview of Eastern and Western Stages of Initiation and Meditation

Standard opening. Call forward Sai Baba, Paramahansa Yogananda and Djwhal Khul to bring forth a group merkabah to take the class to Djwhal Khul's inner-plane ashram. Ask for their guidance, then read chapter 13, "Comparative Overview of Eastern and Western Stages of Initiation and Meditation," from *Cosmic Ascension: Your Cosmic Map Home*. Discuss the material.

Take a break. Play the audio tape, "Ultimate Ascension Activation Meditation," or lead the Ascension Meditation and Treatment beginning on page 45. Personal sharing. Standard closing. Social time.

Class 115
Planetary and Cosmic Discipleship

Standard opening. Call forward Serapis Bey, Hilarion and Djwhal Khul to bring forth a group merkabah to take the class to Serapis Bey's inner-plane ashram and sit in his ascension seat. Ask for their guidance, then take turns reading chapter 14, "Planetary and Cosmic Discipleship," *from Cosmic Ascension: Your Cosmic Map Home*. Discuss the material.

Take a break. Lead the appropriate meditation from the World Service Meditations beginning on page 56. Personal sharing. Standard closing. Social time.

Class 116
Evolvement of Nations

Standard opening. Call forward Lord Buddha, Allah Gobi, Lord Maitreya, Saint Germain and Djwhal Khul to bring forth a group merkabah to take the class to Lord Buddha's inner-plane ashram to sit in his ascension seat. Ask for their guidance, then read chapter 15, "Evolvement of Nations," from *Cosmic Ascension: Your Cosmic Map Home*. Discuss the material.

Take a break. Lead the appropriate meditations from the World Service Meditations beginning on page 56. Personal sharing. Standard closing. Social time.

Class 117
Past Lives of Some Well-Known Ascended Masters

Standard opening. Call forward Buddha, Lord Maitreya and the seven chohans to bring forth a group merkabah to take the class to Lord Maitreya's inner-plane ashram. Ask them for guidance, then take turns reading chapter 11, "Past Lives of Some of the Well-Known Ascended Masters," from *Cosmic Ascension: Your Cosmic Map Home*. Discuss the material.

Take a break. Lead the Cosmic-Ray Meditation beginning on page 31. Personal sharing. Standard closing. Social time.

Class 118
Cosmic Ascension Training

Standard opening. Call forward Melchizedek, the Mahatma and Metatron to bring forth a group merkabah to take the class to Melchizedek's inner-plane ashram to sit in his ascension seat. Ask for their guidance, then read chapter 16, "Cosmic Ascension Training," from *Cosmic Ascension: Your Cosmic Map Home*. Discuss the material.

Take a break. Lead the Meditation in the Golden Chamber of Melchizedek beginning on page 34. Personal sharing. Standard closing. Social time.

Class 119
Synthesis and Integration

Standard opening. Call forward Djwhal Khul and the Mahatma to bring forth a group merkabah to take you to Djwhal Khul's inner-plane ashram. Ask for their guidance during the session, then take turns reading chapter 13, "Synthesis and Integration," from *A Beginner's Guide to the Path of Ascension (Vol. VII)*. Discuss the material.

Take a break. Lead the Meditation in the Golden Chamber of Melchizedek beginning on page 34. Personal sharing. Standard closing. Social time.

Class 120
The Practicality of the Ascension Process

Standard opening. Call forward Djwhal Khul, Kuthumi and Lord Maitreya to bring forth a group merkabah to take you to Kuthumi's inner-plane ashram. Ask for their guidance, then read chapter 7, "The Practicality of the Ascension Process," from *A Beginner's Guide to the Path of Ascension*. Discuss the material.

Take a break. Play the audio tape, "Ultimate Ascension Activation Meditation," or lead the Ascension Meditation and Treatment beginning on page 45. Personal sharing. Standard closing. Social time.

Class 121
Our Animal Brothers and Sisters

Standard opening. Call forward Pan to overlight and guide the class session. Taking turns, read chapter 10, "Our Animal Brothers and Sisters," from *A Beginner's Guide to the Path of Ascension*. Discuss the material and your personal relationship to the animal kingdom.

Take a break. Lead the Specialized Ascension Activations beginning on page 37. Personal sharing. Standard closing. Social time.

Class 122
The True Meaning of Marriage

Standard opening. Call forward the divine Mother, the lady masters—Virgin Mary, Isis, Quan Yin, Vesta, Lakshmi, Pallas Athena—Djwhal Khul and Paul the Venetian to overlight and guide the class. Take turns reading chapter 9, "The True Meaning of Marriage," from *Ascension and Romantic Relationships*. Discuss the material.

Take a break. Lead the Divine Mother and Lady Masters Meditation and Activation beginning on page 52. Personal sharing. Standard closing. Social time.

Class 123
Our Brothers and Sisters of the Stars

Standard opening. Call forward Djwhal Khul, Kuthumi and Lord Maitreya to bring forth a group merkabah to take you to Lord Maitreya's inner-plane ashram. Ask them to guide the session, then read chapter 11, "Our Brothers and Sisters of the Stars," from *A Beginner's Guide to the Path of Ascension*. Discuss the material.

Take a break. Play the audio tape, "God Ascension Seat Journey," or lead the updated version beginning on page 39. Personal sharing. Standard closing. Social time.

Class 124
The Many Lenses of Ascension

Standard opening. Call forward Djwhal Khul, Kuthumi and Lord Maitreya to bring forth a group merkabah to take you to Djwhal Khul's inner-plane ashram. Ask for their guidance, then read chapter 12, "The Many Lenses of Ascension," from *A Beginner's Guide to the Path of Ascension*. Discuss the material.

Take a break. Lead the Ascension Meditation and Treatment beginning on page 45. Personal sharing. Standard closing. Social time.

Class 125
Finding Your Spiritual Mate

Standard opening. Call forward Djwhal Khul, Paul the Venetian and the lady masters—Virgin Mary, Isis, Quan Yin, Vesta, Lakshmi, and Pallas Athena—to bring forth a group merkabah to take you to Paul the Venetian's inner-plane ashram. Ask for their guidance, then take turns reading chapter 1, "Finding Your Mate," from *Ascension and Romantic Relationships*. Discuss the material.

Take a break. Read the Divine Mother and Lady Masters Meditation and Activation beginning on page 52. Personal sharing. Standard closing. Social time.

Class 126
God, the Consummate Union

Standard opening. Call forward the Mahatma, Metatron, the divine Mother, Archangel Michael and Djwhal Khul to overlight and guide the class. Read chapter 10, "God, the Consummate Union," from *Ascension and Romantic Relationships*, then discuss.

Take a break. Play the audio tape, "Updated God Ascension Seat Meditation," or lead it, beginning on page 39. Personal sharing. Standard closing. Social time.

Class 127
Living Your Joy

Standard opening. Call forward Paul the Venetian, Virgin Mary, Quan Yin, Isis and Djwhal Khul to bring forth a group merkabah to take the class to Paul the Venetian's inner-plane ashram. Ask their guidance, then take turns reading chapter 6, "Living Your Joy," from *Your Ascension Mission: Embracing Your Puzzle Piece*. Discuss the material.

Take a break. Lead the guided meditation, Specialized Ascension Activations, beginning on page 37. Personal sharing. Standard closing. Social time.

Class 128
Puzzle Pieces and the 352 Levels of the Mahatma

Standard opening. Call forward the Mahatma and Djwhal Khul to bring forth a group merkabah to take the class to Djwhal Khul's inner-plane ashram. Ask for their guidance, then read chapter 10, "Puzzle Pieces and the 352 Levels of the Mahatma," from *Your Ascension Mission: Embracing Your Puzzle Piece*. Discuss the material.

Take a break. Play the audio tape, "Updated God Ascension Seat Meditation" or lead it, beginning on page 39. Personal sharing. Standard closing. Social time.

Class 129
Spiritual Etiquette

Standard opening. Call forward Saint Germain, El Morya and Djwhal Khul to bring forth a group merkabah to take the class to Saint Germain's inner-plane ashram. Ask for their guidance during the session. Read chapter 11, "Spiritual Etiquette," from *Your Ascension Mission: Embracing Your Puzzle Piece*. Discuss the material.

Take a break. Play the audio tape, "Ultimate Ascension Activation Meditation," or lead the Ascension Meditation and Treatment beginning on page 45. Personal sharing. Standard closing. Social time.

Class 130
The Spiritualization of All Puzzle Pieces

Standard opening. Call forward Melchizedek, the Mahatma, Metatron, the divine Mother, Archangel Michael and Djwhal Khul to bring forth a group merkabah to take the class to Melchizedek's inner-plane ashram to sit in his ascension seat. Ask for their guidance. Then take turns reading chapter 4, "The Spiritualization of All Puzzle Pieces," from *Your Ascension Mission: Embracing Your Puzzle Piece.* Discuss the material.

Take a break. Lead the Meditation in the Golden Chamber of Melchizedek beginning on page 34. Personal sharing. Standard closing. Social time.

Class 131
Relationships, Puzzle Pieces and Ascension Missions

Standard opening. Call forward the divine Mother, Virgin Mary, Quan Yin, Isis, Vesta, Lakshmi, Paul the Venetian and Djwhal Khul to bring forth a group merkabah to take the class to Paul the Venetian's inner-plane ashram. Ask for their guidance, then take turns reading chapter 5, "Relationships, Puzzle Pieces and Ascension Missions," from *Your Ascension Mission: Embracing Your Puzzle Piece.* Discuss the material.

Take a break. Lead the meditation, Divine Mother and the Lady Masters Meditation and Activation, beginning on page 52. Personal sharing. Standard closing. Social time.

Class 132
Blending the Puzzle Pieces

Standard opening. Call forward the Mahatma, Melchizedek, Metatron and Djwhal Khul to bring forth a group merkabah to take the class to Melchizedek's inner-plane ashram to sit in his ascension seat. Ask for their guidance, then take turns reading chapter 7, "Blending the Puzzle Pieces of the Whole," from *Your Ascension Mission: Embracing Your Puzzle Piece.* Discuss the material.

Take a break. Lead the meditations that feel appropriate to the occasion from the World Service Meditations beginning on page 56. Personal sharing. Standard closing. Social time.

Note from the Author

As you work with these class outlines, if you have questions about the classes, books, tapes, manuscripts or the Academy, don't hesitate to contact me at the Melchizedek Synthesis Light Academy & Ashram, 5252 Coldwater Canyon Ave., #112, Van Nuys, California 91401, (818) 769-1181; Fax: (818) 766-1782 or at http://www.drjoshuadavidstone.com.

— Joshua David Stone, Ph.D.

LIGHT TECHNOLOGY PUBLISHING

 7 ### A BEGINNER'S GUIDE
TO THE PATH OF ASCENSION

This volume covers the basics of ascension clearly and completely, from the spiritual hierarchy to the angels and star beings, in Dr. Stone's easy-to-read style. From his background in psychology he offers a unique perspective on such issues as karma, the transcendence of the negative ego, the power of the spoken word and the psychology of ascension.

$14.95   Softcover 166p   ISBN 1-891824-02-3

 8 ### GOLDEN KEYS TO ASCENSION AND HEALING
REVELATIONS OF SAI BABA
AND THE ASCENDED MASTERS

This book represents the wisdom of the ascended masters condensed into concise keys that serve as a spiritual guide. These 420 golden keys present the multitude of methods, techniques, affirmations, prayers and insights Dr. Stone has gleaned from his own background in psychology and life conditions and his thorough research of all the ancient and contemporary classics that speak of the path to God realization.

$14.95   Softcover 206p   ISBN 1-891824-03-1

 9 ### MANUAL FOR PLANETARY LEADERSHIP

Here at last is an indispensable book that has been urgently needed in these uncertain times. This book lays out, in an orderly and clear fashion the guidelines for leadership in the world and in one's own life. It serves as a reference manual for moral and spiritual living and offers a vision of a world where strong love and the highest aspirations of humanity triumph.

$14.95   Softcover 284p   ISBN 1-891824-05-8

 10 ### YOUR ASCENSION MISSION
EMBRACING YOUR PUZZLE PIECE

This book shows how each person's puzzle piece is just as vital and necessary as any other. Fourteen chapters explain in detail all aspects of living the fullest expression of your unique individuality.

$14.95   Softcover 248p   ISBN 1-891824-09-0

 11 ### REVELATIONS OF A MELCHIZEDEK INITIATE

Dr. Stone's spiritual autobiography, beginning with his ascension initiation and progression into the 12th initiation, is filled with insight, tools and information. It will lift you into wondrous planetary and cosmic realms.

$14.95   Softcover   ISBN 1-891824-10-4

 12 ### HOW TO TEACH ASCENSION CLASSES

This book serves as an ideal foundation for teaching ascension classes and presenting workshops. The inner-plane ascended masters have guided Dr. Stone to write this book, using his Easy-to-Read-Encyclopedia of the Spiritual Path as a foundation. It covers an entire one- to two-year program of classes.

$14.95   Softcover 136p   ISBN 1-891824-15-5

THE EXPLORER RACE SERIES

❶ the EXPLORER RACE

This book presents humanity in a new light, as the explorers and problem-solvers of the universe, admired by the other galactic beings for their courage and creativity. Some topics are: **The Genetic Experiment on Earth; The ET in You: Physical Body, Emotion, Thought and Spirit; The Joy, the Glory and the Challenge of Sex; ET Perspectives; The Order: Its Origin and Resolution; Coming of Age in the Fourth Dimension and much more!**

574p $25.00

❷ ETs and the EXPLORER RACE

In this book Robert channels Joopah, a Zeta Reticulan now in the ninth dimension, who continues the story of the great experiment — the Explorer Race — from the perspective of his race. The Zetas would have been humanity's future selves had not humanity re-created the past and changed the future.
237p $14.95

❸ Origins and the Next 50 Years

Some chapters are: **THE ORIGINS OF EARTH RACES:** Our Creator and Its Creation, The White Race and the Andromedan Linear Mind, The Asian Race, The African Race, The Fairy Race and the Native Peoples of the North, The Australian Aborigines, The Origin of Souls. **THE NEXT 50 YEARS:** The New Corporate Model, The Practice of Feeling, Benevolent Magic, Future Politics, A Visit to the Creator of All Creators. **ORIGINS OF THE CREATOR:** Creating with Core Resonances; Jesus, the Master Teacher; Recent Events in Explorer Race History; On Zoosh, Creator and the Explorer Race. 339p $14.95

THE EXPLORER RACE SERIES

④ EXPLORER RACE: Creators and Friends — the Mechanics of Creation

As we explore the greater reality beyond our planet, our galaxy, our dimension, our creation, we meet prototypes, designers, shapemakers, creators, creators of creators and friends of our Creator, who explain their roles in this creation and their experiences before and beyond this creation. As our awareness expands about the way creation works, our awareness of who we are expands and we realize that a part of ourselves is in that vast creation — and that we are much greater and more magnificent than even science fiction had led us to believe. Join us in the adventure of discovery. It's mind-stretching!

435p $19.95

⑤ EXPLORER RACE: Particle Personalities

All around you in every moment you are surrounded by the most magical and mystical beings. They are too small for you to see as single individuals, but in groups you know them as the physical matter of your daily life. Particles who might be considered either atoms or portions of atoms consciously view the vast spectrum of reality, yet also have a sense of personal memory like your own linear memory. These particles remember where they have been and what they have done in their infinitely long lives. Some of the particles we hear from are Gold, Mountain Lion, Liquid Light, Uranium, the Great Pyramid's Capstone, This Orb's Boundary, Ice and Ninth-Dimensional Fire. 237p $14.95

⑥ EXPLORER RACE: EXPLORER RACE and BEYOND

In our continuing exploration of how creation works, we talk to Creator of Pure Feelings and Thoughts, the Liquid Domain, the Double-Diamond Portal, and the other 93% of the Explorer Race. We revisit the Friends of the Creator to discuss their origin and how they see the beyond; we finally reach the root seeds of the Explorer Race (us!) and find we are from a different source than our Creator and have a different goal; and we end up talking to All That Is! 360p $14.95

EXPLORER

RACE

AND BEYOND

Explorer Race Roots, Friends, and All That Is with Zoosh through Robert Shapiro

AVAILABLE MID-1998 . . .

⑦ EXPLORER RACE and ISIS

Isis sets the record straight on her interaction with humans — what she set out to do and what actually happened. $14.95

COMING SOON

Ⓐ EXPLORER RACE: Material Mastery Series

Secret shamanic techniques to heal particular energy points on Earth, which then feeds healing energy back to humans. $14.95

Former U.S. Naval
Intelligence Briefing Team
Member reveals
information kept secret by
our government since the
1940s. UFOs, the J.F.K.
assassination, the Secret
Government, the war on
drugs and more
by the world's leading
expert on UFOs.

Behold A Pale Horse

About the Author

Bill Cooper, former United States Naval Intelligence Briefing Team member, reveals information that remains hidden from the public eye. This information has been kept in top-secret government files since the 1940s.

In 1988 Bill decided to "talk" due to events then taking place worldwide. Since Bill has been "talking," he has correctly predicted the lowering of the Iron Curtain, the fall of the Berlin Wall and the invasion of Panama, all of record well before the events occurred. His information comes from top-secret documents that he read while with the Intelligence Briefing Team and from over 17 years of thorough research.

by
William Cooper

$25.00
Softcover 500p
ISBN 0-929385-22-5

Excerpt from pg. 94

"I read while in Naval Intelligence that at least once a year, maybe more, two nuclear submarines meet beneath the polar icecap and mate together at an airlock. Representatives of the Soviet Union meet with the Policy Committee of the Bilderberg Group. The Russians are given the script for their next performance. Items on the agenda include the combined efforts in the secret space program governing Alternative 3. I now have in my possession official NASA photographs of a moon base in the crater Copernicus."

Table of Contents